MAPPING SOCIAL NETWORKS, SPATIAL DATA, & HIDDEN POPULATIONS

ETHNOGRAPHER'S TOOLKIT

Edited by Jean J. Schensul, *Institute for Community Research, Hartford,* and
Margaret D. LeCompte, *School of Education, University of Colorado, Boulder*

The **Ethnographer's Toolkit** is designed with you, the novice fieldworker, in mind. In a series
of seven brief books, the editors and authors of the **Toolkit** take you through the multiple,
complex steps of doing ethnographic research in simple, reader-friendly language. Case
studies, checklists, key points to remember, and additional resources to consult are all included
to help the reader fully understand the ethnographic process. Eschewing a step-by-step
formula approach, the authors are able to explain the complicated tasks and relationships that
occur in the field in clear, helpful ways. Research designs, data collection techniques, analytical
strategies, research collaborations, and an array of uses for ethnographic work in policy,
programming, and practice are described in the volumes. The **Toolkit** is the perfect starting
point for professionals in diverse fields including social welfare, education, health, economic
development, and the arts, as well as for advanced students and experienced researchers unfamiliar with the demands of conducting good ethnography.

Summer 1999/7 volumes/paperback boxed set/0-7619-9042-9

BOOKS IN THE ETHNOGRAPHER'S TOOLKIT

1. **Designing and Conducting Ethnographic Research,** by Margaret D. LeCompte and
   Jean J. Schensul, 0-7619-8975-7 (paperback)

2. **Essential Ethnographic Methods: Observations, Interviews, and Questionnaires,**
   by Stephen Schensul, Jean J. Schensul, and Margaret D. LeCompte, 0-7619-9144-1
   (paperback)

3. **Enhanced Ethnographic Methods: Audiovisual Techniques, Focused Group Interviews,
   and Elicitation Techniques,** by Jean J. Schensul, Margaret D. LeCompte,
   Bonnie K. Nastasi, and Stephen P. Borgatti, 0-7619-9129-8 (paperback)

4. **Mapping Social Networks, Spatial Data, and Hidden Populations,** by Jean J. Schensul,
   Margaret D. LeCompte, Robert T. Trotter II, Ellen K. Cromley, and Merrill Singer,
   0-7619-9112-3 (paperback)

5. **Analyzing and Interpreting Ethnographic Data,** by Margaret D. LeCompte and
   Jean J. Schensul, 0-7619-8974-9 (paperback)

6. **Researcher Roles and Research Partnerships,** by Margaret D. LeCompte,
   Jean J. Schensul, Margaret R. Weeks, and Merrill Singer, 0-7619-8973-0 (paperback)

7. **Using Ethnographic Data: Interventions, Public Programming, and Public Policy,**
   by Jean J. Schensul, Margaret D. LeCompte, G. Alfred Hess, Jr., Bonnie K. Nastasi,
   Marlene J. Berg, Lynne Williamson, Jeremy Brecher, and Ruth Glasser, 0-7619-8972-2
   (paperback)

MAPPING SOCIAL NETWORKS, SPATIAL DATA, & HIDDEN POPULATIONS

JEAN J. SCHENSUL
MARGARET D. LeCOMPTE
ROBERT T. TROTTER II
ELLEN K. CROMLEY
MERRILL SINGER

4 ETHNOGRAPHER'S TOOLKIT

A Division of Sage Publications, Inc.
Walnut Creek ◆ London ◆ New Delhi

For information:

AltaMira Press
A Division of Sage Publications, Inc.
1630 North Main Street, Suite 367
Walnut Creek, California 94596 USA
explore@altamira.sagepub.com
E-mail: http:\www.altamirapress.com

Sage Publications, Ltd.
6 Bonhill Street
London, EC2A 4PU
United Kingdom

Sage Publications India Pvt. Ltd.
M-32 Market
Greater Kailash I
New Delhi 100 048
India

Printed in the United States of America

Library of Congress Cataloging-in-Publication Data

Schensul, Jean J.
    Mapping social networks, spatial data, and hidden populations /
by Jean J. Schensul and Margaret D. LeCompte, Robert T. Trotter II,
Ellen K. Cromley, and Merrill Singer.
        p. cm. — (Ethnographer's toolkit; v. 4)
    Includes bibliographical references and index.
    ISBN 0-7619-9112-3 (pbk.: alk. paper)
    1. Ethnology—Research   2. Social networks—Research.
3. Spatial behavior—Research.   I. LeCompte, Margaret Diane.
II. Trotter, Robert T.   III. Cromley, Ellen K.   IV. Singer, Merrill.
V. Title. VI. Series.
    GN345.S363   1999
    305.8'007'2—ddc21   98-40072

This book is printed on acid-free paper.

99 00 01 02 03 10 9 8 7 6 5 4 3 2 1

Production Editor: Astrid Virding
Editorial Assistant: Denise Santoyo
Designer/Typesetter: Janelle LeMaster
Cover Designer: Ravi Balasuriya
Cover Artist: Ed Johnetta Miller, Graciela Quiñones Rodriguez

CONTENTS

Introduction   vii
   Jean J. Schensul and Margaret D. LeCompte

1. Friends, Relatives, and Relevant Others: Conducting Ethnographic
   Network Studies   1
      Robert T. Trotter, II

   Introduction to Network Research   1
   Key Concepts for Ethnographic Approaches to Social Networks   8
   Ego-Centered Approaches to Understanding Networks   18
   Full Network Relationships: Reciprocal Network Information   30
   Network Sampling Strategies   38
   Summary and Conclusions   41
   Notes   47
   References   48
   Suggested Resources   49

2. Mapping Spatial Data   51
      Ellen K. Cromley

   The Spatial Perspective   51
   Spatial Dimensions of Community   54
   Spatial Dimensions of Individual Life   66
   Collecting Data on Activity Spaces   72
   Implications of Activity Data Collection for Analysis   80
   Spatial Dimensions of Community Institutions   83

101505

Spatial Sampling   94
Mapping Spatial Data   97
The Power of Maps   117
References   119
Suggested Resources   123

3. Studying Hidden Populations   125
   Merrill Singer

   What Are Hidden Populations?   125
   Evolution of Hidden Population Research   135
   Recruiting Study Participants   159
   Methodological Considerations   169
   Ethical Issues   181
   Conclusions   188
   References   189
   Suggested Resources   191

   Index   193

   About the Authors, Artists, and Editors   201

INTRODUCTION

The **Ethnographer's Toolkit** is a series of texts on how to plan, design, carry out, and use the results of applied ethnographic research. Ethnography, as an approach to research, may be unfamiliar to people accustomed to more traditional forms of research, but we believe that applied ethnography will prove not only congenial but essential to both researchers and practitioners. Many kinds of evaluative or investigative questions that arise in the course of program planning and implementation cannot really be answered very well with standard research methods such as experiments or collection of quantifiable data alone. Often, there are no data yet to quantify nor programs whose effectiveness needs to be assessed! Sometimes, the research problem to be addressed is not yet clearly identified and must be discovered. In such cases, ethnographic research provides a valid and important way to find out what *is* happening in programs and to help practitioners plan their activities.

This book series defines what ethnographic research is, when it should be used, and how it can be used to identify and solve complex social problems, especially those not readily amenable to traditional quantitative or experimental research methods alone. It is designed for educators; service professionals; professors of applied students in the fields of teaching, social and health services, communications, engineering, and business; and students working in applied field settings.

Ethnography is a peculiarly human endeavor. Many of its practitioners have commented that, unlike other approaches to research, the *researcher* is the primary tool for collecting primary data. That is, as Books 1, 2, 3, and 4 demonstrate, the ethnographer's principal database is amassed in the course of human interaction: direct observation; face-to-face interviewing and elicitation; audiovisual recording; and mapping the networks, times, and places in which human interactions occur. Thus, as Book 6 makes clear, the personal characteristics and activities of researchers as human beings and as scientists become salient in ways not applicable in research where the investigator maintains more distance from the people and phenomena under study.

Book 1 of the **Ethnographer's Toolkit,** *Designing and Conducting Ethnographic Research,* defines what ethnographic research is and the predominant viewpoints or paradigms that guide ethnography. It provides the reader with an overview of research methods and design, including how to develop research questions, what to consider in setting up the mechanics of a research project, and how to devise a sampling plan. Ways of collecting and analyzing data, and the ethical considerations for which ethnographers must account, conclude this overall introduction to the series. In Book 2 of the **Ethnographer's Toolkit,** titled *Essential Ethnographic Methods,* readers are provided with an introduction to participant and nonparticipant observation, interviewing, and ethnographically informed survey research, including systematically administered structured interviews and questionnaires. These data collection strategies are fundamental to good ethnographic research. The essential methods provide ethnographers with tools to answer the principal ethnographic questions: "What's happening in this setting?" "Who is engaging in what kind of activities?" and "Why are they doing what they are doing?" Ethnographers use these tools to enter a field situation and obtain basic information about social structure, social events, cultural patterns, and the meanings that people give to these patterns. The essential tools also permit ethnographers to learn about new situations from the perspective of insiders because they require ethnographers to become involved in the local cultural setting and to acquire their knowledge through hands-on experience.

In Book 3, *Enhanced Ethnographic Methods,* the reader adds to this basic inventory of ethnographic tools three different but important approaches to data collection, each one a complement to the essential methods presented in Book 2. These tools are audiovisual techniques, focused group interviews, and elicitation techniques. We have termed these data collection strategies "enhanced ethnographic methods" because each of them parallels and enhances a strategy first presented in Book 2.

Audiovisual techniques, which involve recording behavior and speech using electronic equipment, expand the capacity of ethnographers to observe and listen by creating a more complete and permanent record of events and speech. Focused group interviews permit ethnographers to interview more than one person at a time. Elicitation techniques allow ethnographers to quantify qualitative or perceptual data on how individuals and groups of people think about and organize perceptions of their cultural world.

It is important for the reader to recognize that, although the essential ethnographic methods described in Book 2 can be used alone, the enhanced ethnographic methods covered in Book 3 cannot, by themselves, provide a fully rounded picture of cultural life in a community, organization, work group, school, or other setting. Instead, they must be used in combination with the essential methods outlined in Book 2. Doing so adds dimensions of depth and accuracy to the cultural portrait constructed by the ethnographer.

Book 5, *Analyzing and Interpreting Ethnographic Data,* provides the reader with a variety of methods for transforming piles of fieldnotes, observations, audio- and videotapes, questionnaires, surveys, documents, maps, and other kinds of data into research results that help people to understand their world more fully and facilitate problem solving. Addressing both narrative and qualitative, as well as quantitative—or enumerated—data, Book 5 discusses methods for organizing, retrieving, rendering manageable, and interpreting the data collected in ethnographic research.

In Book 6, *Researcher Roles and Research Partnerships,* we discuss the special requirements that doing ethnographic research imposes on its practitioners. Throughout the toolkit, we have argued that there is little difference between the exercise of ethnography as a systematic and scientific enterprise and applied ethnography as that same systematic and scientific enterprise used specifically for helping people identify and solve human problems. To that end, in Chapter 1, "Researcher Roles," we first describe how the work of ethnographers is inextricably tied to the type of person the ethnographer is, the particular social and cultural context of the research site, and the tasks and responsibilities that ethnographers assume in the field.

In the second chapter, "Building Research Partnerships," we recognize that ethnography seldom is done by lone researchers. We discuss how ethnographers assemble research teams, establish partnerships with individuals and institutions in the field, and work collaboratively with a wide range of people and organizations to solve mutually identified problems. The chapter concludes with ethical and procedural considerations, including developing social and managerial infrastructure, establishing and breaking contracts, negotiating different organizational cultures and values, and resolving conflicts.

The final book in the series, *Using Ethnographic Data,* consists of three chapters that present general guidelines and case studies illustrating how ethnographers have used ethnographic data in planning public programs, developing and evaluating interventions, and influencing public policy.

Throughout the series, authors give examples drawn from their own work and the work of their associates. These examples and case studies present ways in which ethnographers have coped with the kinds of problems and dilemmas found in the field—and described in the series—in the course of their work and over extended periods of time.

Readers less familiar with ethnographic research will gain an introduction to basic ethnographic principles, methods, and techniques by reading Books 1, 2, 5, and 6 first, followed by other books that explore more specialized areas of research and use. Those familiar with basic ethnographic methods will find Books 3, 4, and 7 valuable in enhancing their repertoires of research methods, data collection techniques, and ways of approaching the use of ethnographic data in policy and program settings.

In Book 4, *Mapping Social Networks, Spatial Data, and Hidden Populations,* we add to the enhanced methods of data collection and analysis used by ethnographers. However, the approach taken in Book 4 is informed by a somewhat different perspective on the way social life is organized in communities. Whereas the previous books focus primarily on ways of understanding cultural patterns and the interactions of individuals and groups in cultural settings, Book 4 focuses on social and what we term "sociogeographic" space.

We believe that these three chapters address related issues: mapping and identifying how and with whom people interact; and mapping how the organizations and structures with which people interact, and that they create in their interactions, are arrayed in geographic space. We have already suggested that people do not react only as individuals; rather, they *interact* with each other in groups. However, most social or cultural groups interact within the context of *events,* which themselves occur in a specific location, within specific environmental conditions, and at a specific point in time. Events can range from community health fairs and rock music concerts to meetings of drug abusers or community-based artists. They can include visits to a market, school, needle exchange van, beauty salon, or public water tap. They also encompass conversations ranging from street corner conversations under a shade tree to discussions among policy-oriented environmentalists at a professional conference. Understanding these events requires knowing something about who the people involved in such events are, where they come from, why they are in attendance, and whether or not they are acquainted with other participants in the event.

Readers can think about these matters by considering who the *individuals* involved in events are and whether their personal social networks—or their intimate personal friends and family—affect how they use space and time. For example, friends may influence whether someone attends a school theater performance or football game. A second way to think about these matters is to consider how *individuals relate to one another.* For example, do close or intimate friends influence a teenager to take a puff on a cigarette? The relationship here may be characterized by degree of intimacy and what the individuals *do* together. A third considers the relationships among *social events themselves,* locations or organizations, and how *individuals relate to these events.* For example, specific groups or organizations may work together on a project, such as an AIDS prevention program in which some people, but not all, participate. Network analysis and social mapping, two of the topics covered in Book 4, provide readers with the conceptual frameworks and research technologies to study and analyze the structure of groups and communities in the ways outlined above. The third topic, outlined in Chapter 3, addresses the challenges of conducting research with hidden populations. To do so, it draws on methods and approaches used in network research and sociogeographic mapping, as well as essential ethnographic methods, to define and bound research populations; gain entry into groups of people involved in stigmatized, marginalized, dangerous, or illegal activities; and recruit them into appropriate studies.

The first chapter in Book 4 uses several extended case examples to demonstrate that social networks consisting of interconnected individuals can be viewed from the perspective of both the individual respondent and the community. The personal networks of individual respondents—the people who are identified as important to them—and the full relational networks—networks of individuals linked together in a definable community—can be described both ethnographically and quantitatively.

The chapter opens with ways of identifying and defining networks using the ethnographic methods of observation and interviews outlined in Books 2 and 3. It also discusses the way human beings use social networks. It then defines "ego-centered" and "full relational" networks, discusses their functions for human beings, and gives examples of how data are collected and used both to better understand how social networks function and affect people, and to use that information for more effective intervention programs. Readers will be introduced to sample questionnaires and data collection forms that they can use as models for their own work. Additional readings and computerized tools for data collection and analysis are listed in the Suggested Resources section at the end of the chapter.

The second chapter in Book 4 moves readers from social relationships to the location of these relationships in geographic space. The author points out that most things that interest ethnographers are, in fact, located in, influenced by, and even constrained by geographic factors. She tells us that "spatial analysis of geographic data is concerned with the relationships among individuals or other objects located on the earth's surface—in particular, those relationships that vary when the locations of the objects change."

The chapter first provides a frame of reference for thinking about communities and individuals in geographic space and how to consider and collect data on ways that individuals use and are influenced by geographic space. It then demonstrates how communities can be though of as collections of "institutions" that, like individuals, are related to one another in both social and geographic space. It also presents ways of collecting and analyzing data on institutional relationships. Concluding the chapter are suggestions for sampling and a discussion of how maps can be used effectively as analytic tools to tell stories about the spatial relationship between people and community resources, and to interpret the meaning of such stories.

Chapter 3 introduces readers to the concept of the "hidden population." Because of their skills in gaining unobtrusive access to communities and other settings, ethnographers have often been called upon to find and do research with people who, for economic, political, legal, or other reasons, are not readily identified. More often than not, by virtue of their status and behavior, such people may not wish to be identified. The chapter defines hidden populations and discusses the history of work on hidden populations, especially in the areas of drug use and, more recently, HIV research. The evolution and main defining characteristics of models used by research teams in cities across the United States are described. The remainder of the chapter examines strategies for defining hidden populations so that they can be sampled for research purposes and for recruitment as study participants.

Many studies that draw upon participants from hidden populations are cross-sectional, that is, they are designed to take place at one point in time. Others may involve small samples whose members have a personal relationship with the ethnographer and continue their associations over time. In both instances, the challenge is to identify a large enough sample to meet the constraints of the cross-sectional design. Increasingly, however, injection drug users, gang members, commercial sex workers, school dropouts, women who are victims of violence, and others have become the focus for supportive intervention strategies. In such instances, longitudinal designs that call for interviews at two points in time are critical. One contribution of this chapter is its discussion of the problem of bias that occurs in carrying out panel studies or longitudinal designs with people who are difficult to reach in the first place and difficult to locate repeatedly over time.

Finally, research with hidden populations raises many ethical considerations. People who are hard to reach often have overwhelming personal or family needs and may call upon ethnographers for assistance. Ethnographers who establish close personal relationships with research participants feel compelled to respond. In such instances, researchers may be asked to participate in illegal or dangerous activities and must be able to define the boundaries of what is appropriate in the field and in the context of their relationships with others. Research participants may live in dangerous circumstances, exposing researchers to circumstances of exposure to violence, theft, and personal loss. These issues are addressed in the final section of this important chapter.

—Jean J. Schensul and Margaret D. LeCompte

1

FRIENDS, RELATIVES, AND RELEVANT OTHERS: CONDUCTING ETHNOGRAPHIC NETWORK STUDIES

Robert T. Trotter II

Introduction to Network Research

•

Key Concepts for Ethnographic Approaches to Social Networks

•

Ego-Centered Approaches to Understanding Networks

•

Full Network Relationships: Reciprocal Network Information

•

Network Sampling Strategies

•

Summary and Conclusions

INTRODUCTION TO NETWORK RESEARCH

There is a Spanish proverb that states, "Di me con quien andan, y dire quien eres," which generally translates as "Tell me who you walk with, and I will tell you who you are." We all reflect our values and beliefs, as well as our hopes and accomplishments, through the people with whom we choose to associate and those whom we avoid. Our social world is made up primarily of our family and friends, work partners, acquaintances, and the organizations and communities in which we participate. Anthropologists have studied the composition of these relationships, or **social networks,** in villages, towns, and urban centers all over the world. Social scientists most frequently

Definition:
A social network is a specific type of relation linking a defined set of people, organizations, or communities

AUTHOR'S NOTE: Funding for much of the research reported in this chapter was provided by two grants from the National Institute on Drug Abuse (NIDA). These were Grant #U01-DA07295, the Flagstaff Multicultural AIDS Prevention Project, and Grant #R01 DA09965, Small Town Drug Networks and HIV: Transmission Dynamics.

1

have used studies of social networks for two purposes: to identify the members of and patterns of interaction among groups of various kinds, including friendship, work, and kinship groups; and to select respondents or participants for a research study by identifying people who know or know about each other. The latter procedure is called "network sampling" and is described in Books 1 and 2.

Cross Reference: See Book 1, Book 2, Chapter 9, and Book 4, Chapter 3, for more information on network sampling

Today, however, the social network approach has been put to use for more sophisticated purposes. Once ethnographers noticed how group structures differ within and between cultures, and began to question how these differences might influence what people think and do, network research gained importance in understanding and predicting individual knowledge, behavior, and beliefs. Differences in the ways in which organizations are structured, as well as in the positions people occupy within them, affect the flow of information, constraining not only the amount but the specific content of information that people receive. Studies of social networks allow social scientists to explore cultural differences in the ways that humans organize themselves into groups, communicate about critical life circumstances, and work out the problems they encounter in everyday life. This information can be used to very good effect in studies as widely different as explorations of drug use patterns, analyses of why parents choose particular schools for their children, or investigations into the reasons people do or do not welcome agricultural innovations.

In this chapter, we use an extended case example to describe the use of ethnographic network analysis. In our case example, network analysis was instrumental in identifying various kinds of drug user networks; it also illuminated how different patterns of behavior among the drug users within specific networks are affected by the different bases or purposes upon which the networks are based. Although the extended example used in this chapter is drawn from medical anthropology, the techniques used in this study could be applied to the study of any kind of social network. Typical applications of social network research might include studies of the implementation of educational innovations, shifts in voting behavior or diffusion of health care information in a community, and reorganization or restructuring of bureaucratic institutions. We believe that such studies are particularly useful for intervention programs whose purpose is to induce change in how a particular group of people behaves.

Two different approaches to understanding cultural networks are important in ethnographic research. The first, systematic exploration of kinship groups, was summarized by Pasternak (1976). The second, ethnographic exploration of social networks, was spelled out by Elizabeth Bott (1971) in studies she conducted in England. These two works represent anchor points for ethnographically framed social network analysis. The first describes methods for collecting data on, and comparing the ways that different cultures identify, genealogical relationships. The second provides both in-depth exploration of the intimate or personal support networks that most people use to survive in their culture, and a model for exploring these relationships across cultures. Following these studies, anthropologists have crafted increasingly fine-tuned examinations of both informal and formal human groups and associations (Galaskiewicz & Wasserman, 1993; Johnson, 1994; Wasserman & Faust, 1993). These works have allowed us to expand our knowledge of the dynamics and effects of both kinship and nonkinship networks in all aspects of human cultures.

There are a number of ways to approach social network research in ethnographic studies. These range from the purely qualitative descriptions of groups and associations to highly technical quantitative models derived from graph theory and matrix algebra. These approaches are compatible with each other, and each provides valuable insights into human cultures. In combination, they provide powerful explanations for the ways in which humans think, act, and organize their daily lives within their personal cultural context. The same approaches described in this chapter for describing and analyzing social networks consisting of individuals can be applied to networks consisting of organizations such as service agencies, towns, cities, and larger social entities. The three primary contemporary approaches to networks are the following:

Cross Reference: For more information on network analysis involving larger social units, see Book 4, Chapter 2

1. The ethnographic exploration of social networks
2. The investigation of ego-centered (single-person-focused) networks
3. The collection of data on full relational networks, where each person describes his or her relationship with each other person in the network

Ethnographic Network Mapping

Definition: Ethnographic network mapping uses ethnographic field research methods to describe the most common groups found in a culture

We first describe **ethnographic network mapping,** a type of network research that can be used to describe family groups, friendship networks, work groups, voluntary associations, problem-solving groups, and any other types of social groups that are found in different cultures. Ethnographic network mapping is accomplished through extensive qualitative interviewing at the community level, combined with observations of people's behavior. An example of this approach currently in use in medical anthropology is the study of drug-using networks (Friedman, 1995; Latkin, 1995; Trotter, Bowen, & Potter, 1995). These drug networks are groups whose primary purpose is purchasing, distributing, and using illegal drugs. The ethnographic description of these networks includes the following:

■ The identity of people in them
■ How people define or self-define themselves as group members
■ The rules people use for including and excluding members

- Familial and sexual relationships within the groups
- Information about how group members avoid the police and prosecution

These are, of course, only a few of the interactions that occur within such groups, and between these groups and others, such as the police and other drug traffickers. Ethnographic network studies provide descriptions of the individual and group cultural context of drug use (such as crack houses, local manufacturing and distribution systems, or police approaches to drug busts) and create typologies or classifications of different types of drug use networks. These studies are very useful for understanding group-based differences in drug use and creating targeted intervention and education activities for the highest risk groups (Trotter, Bowen, & Potter, 1995). Classic gang studies also use the concept of ethnographic networks, considering differences in group organization and functions, and changes in groups in space and over generations.

Ego-Centered or Personal Network Research

The second approach to network research focuses on ego-centered (personal) networks. Studies based on this approach describe index or focal individuals (often called egos) and all of the people (sometimes called "alters") whom these index individuals identify as being associated with them. The data collected on personal networks usually include information about the size of the network, as well as the gender and ethnic composition, age, and socioeconomic attributes of all of the people that egos name as being close to themselves. This allows the researcher to describe "typical" network profiles. These profiles can be related to an infinite variety of other characteristics (level of social support in a specific cultural area, success in personal relationships, risks for infection, quality of life,

Definition:
Ego-centered networks are the personal networks of individuals, also called "egos" or "focal individuals"

Definition:
"Alters" are those people whom index individuals (egos) identify as members of their personal networks

educational attainment, types of help-seeking behavior that members use regarding their health, ideas about success in the future, etc.) that are associated with people's lives. One result of ego-centered network research is that it gives ethnographers the ability to describe the context of people's lives beyond their individual social and psychological characteristics. These contextual elements can be treated as variables and then used to describe the ego's network characteristics, much as demographic variables such as sex, age, political affiliation, and ethnicity describe individual egos.

Full Relational Social Networks

Definition: A full relational social network is a socially bounded group in which the relationships of all members to each other can be defined

Definition: A naturally occurring social network is one that exists and interacts in a specific setting independent of researcher intervention

The third approach to network research is the study of **full relational social networks,** which requires different analysis procedures (Knoke & Kuklinski, 1982). This approach requires the researcher to identify a **naturally occurring social network** and to explore key relationships among and between all of the members of the network. This is accomplished by either observations or interviewing, or a combination of the two. The questions or the observations are designed to allow the ethnographer to explore reciprocal actions that potentially take place between each member of the network and each other member. All of the questions asked, and the observations conducted, focus on questions about relationships that are phrased in terms of what respondents are doing with one another, such as, "Who attends social events with each other?" "Who trusts whom?" and "Who shares food, space, or ideas with whom?" and discovering through additional inquiry more about the question. For example, ethnographers might ask, "Which social events occur?" "What purposes do these events have?" and "What do people do together there?" These questions usually can be qualitative—that is, they are phrased as open-ended or semistructured questions if the social network is small enough for the researcher to conduct in-depth interviews with all of the members. Larger networks (10 people or more) call for quantitative interviews and could include such specific questions as "Did you ever share a needle with X?" (answer yes or no) or "How many times in the past 30 days did you share a needle with X?" (answer in absolute numbers).

These relationship questions allow researchers to

- Explore both the actual and potential connections between people in the network
- Describe the primary sources of power, influence, and communication in a network
- Find **subgroups** within the network
- Identify common or unusual social roles and positions in the networks
- Find **bridges** between networks and portions of networks
- Identify and compare the overall structure of one social network with others

The results of these studies can be used in a number of practical solutions to human problems by identifying people or organizations who can influence the behavior of the remainder of the network in some desired fashion, or by making use of the social network itself to set group goals and change group norms in relation to behaviors that are to be modified.

The social network approach allows ethnographers to move beyond the level of the individual and the analysis of individual behavior into the social context where most people spend the vast majority of their lives, living and interacting with the small groups that make up the world around them.

Cross Reference:
See Book 2, Chapters 6, 7, and 8, for more detailed information

Definition:
Subgroups are subunits within a larger network that are distinctive because the people or units in them are more strongly interconnected with each other compared with other parts of the network

Definition:
Bridges are people or organizations that connect two networks

KEY CONCEPTS FOR ETHNOGRAPHIC
APPROACHES TO SOCIAL NETWORKS

 Key point *Ethnographic studies of sociocultural networks are needed in almost all areas of life.* Some of the most common subjects for these studies include the following:

- *Defining the boundaries and core participants* of social groups
- *Creating network typologies* that explain the variation in people's life experiences
- *Studying embedded behaviors* (the things that go on in specific groups)
- *Exploring cross-group differences* in the cultural behavior of networks

 Cross Reference: For a definition of culture, see Book 1

Boundaries and Bridges

 Definition: Boundaries constitute the edges of networks and are defined by rules for entry and exit from groups as well as by other cultural patterns of participation that differentiate one group from another

Understanding the existence of and being able to identify **boundaries,** the "edges of networks," and bridges are central to any understanding of both small and large groups. Ethnographic techniques, including direct, long-term observation of behavior and relationships, provide important clues to the formation maintenance, change, and dissolution of network boundaries and the identity and functions of people or groups of people who serve as bridges between networks.

 Cross Reference: See Book 2, Chapters 5 and 6, for more information on observation and open-ended interviewing

The mechanisms that allow a group to get together, identify itself as a group, maintain an identity (even with changes in membership over time), and eventually loosen its boundaries and disappear can all be explored descriptively through observation and open-ended interviewing. Ethnographic documentation shows that these conditions change according to key environmental and cultural conditions, such as population density, gender differences, and cultural values and beliefs. Once **bounded groups** have been identified, it is possible to determine how interpersonal connections are created between different people and

Definition: Bounded groups are networks with clearly defined membership

groups of people, and to understand the strength of the links between network members.

The ethnographic study of bridges and boundaries helps social scientists understand both the cognitive models of roles held by network members and the indigenous understandings of the conditions that produce and maintain boundaries at the edges of networks. For example, detailed qualitative description of the behavior and function of boundaries and bridges between networks can be used to create a model of how vulnerable different types of networks are to infectious disease risk. This type of description also can show how a teenage fad is transmitted throughout a high school, or be used to trace a technological innovation through a culture.

Network Typologies

Ethnographers can use typologies of networks or descriptions of different kinds of networks as useful tools for understanding some of the cultural variations that exist within any group. Different types of networks may be focused on a particular problem, a resource, an idea, or a social condition. For example, lifestyle groupings such as the following can typically be found among teenagers in most high schools in the United States; they clearly reflect different behaviors and interests:

- Skaters
- Jocks and cheerleaders
- Drug users
- Preppies
- Dweebs and nerds

Ethnographers generate typologies by looking for the terms that people use to define such natural groupings, identifying common behaviors that cut across groups, and describing relationships within and between groups. The groupings listed above represent only one kind of typology of peer groups in high school settings. Typologies advance our understanding of the important social relationships that exist in networks. They can be used to generate hypotheses about social groups that can be tested in other studies. They allow us to classify differences among social networks based on conditions such as the amount of time people spend with relatives, the types of economic exchanges in which people engage, the risks people are willing to take, or any other set of social conditions that is important for understanding a culture.

An example of how a typological study can be carried out comes from the Flagstaff Multicultural AIDS Prevention Program (FMAPP). In this study, we asked a series of questions guided by structural characteristics of networks. Terms that we used to describe networks are defined in the margin.

Case Study
FMAPP project

The purpose of the FMAPP project was to find new ways to reduce the transmission of HIV among active drug users. Some of the questions that the researchers asked elicited information on the following:

- How long people had been using drugs
- What drugs they used
- Why they were using drugs
- What kinds of risks they were taking (especially those risks that might lead to HIV infection)
- What their own drug-using networks' characteristics were

The purpose of these questions was to provide an overview of local drug use and drug-using groups. One of the first uses of our ethnographic network mapping was to develop a drug networks classification or typology to see if risks varied across different kinds of networks. Our ethnographic interviews indicated that there were three major structural conditions that differed among the various drug networks. These were the following:

- The openness versus the closed condition of networks
- The types of social bonds present in the groups
- The different kinds of social interactions that existed between network participants

We measured the **openness** of the networks by the number of new members recruited over time, combined with the length of time it takes for someone to join a network from the outside. An open network is one that has a high percentage of newly or recently recruited members; a closed network is one that does not allow the recruitment of new members to any significant degree over time.

The types and the number of **social bonds** we identified across different groups include kinship relations, long-term friendships, shorter term acquaintanceships, and weak or close-to-anonymous relationships. A single drug-using group may include all or only some of these relationships.

The third variable we used to construct our classification was the type and amount of **social interactions** (or activities) that exist within networks, such as group drug use, joint recreational activities, or work-related associations. Joint drug use, in particular, is a key social activity for these groups. For this variable, we defined at one end of the continuum the absence of any joint social activities for the group as a whole. Moving away from this end of the continuum, the next level of interaction we observed was face-to-face activities limited to dyads or triads in the group. The far end of the activity continuum included a high level of social interaction, including parties, participation in softball leagues, and other recreational activities involving the entire group.

Our ethnographic network data combined these three structural domains to produce a typology with four distinct, internally consistent, and externally divergent kinds of drug networks. These were the following:

- Long-term injector networks
- Family-based drug networks

Definition: The openness/ closedness of networks refers to the number of new members recruited during a designated period of time

Definition: Social bond refers to the type of relationship between ego and other members of the network. Social bonds may be multiple and weak versus limited and strong

Definition: Social inter-actions refer to activities in which network members participate together

- Friendship-based networks
- Convenience networks

We found that *long-term injector networks* often included individuals from a variety of social, economic, and ethnic backgrounds. The primary purpose of such a group was to pool resources for the acquisition of drugs. Joint drug use activities did not extend very much beyond "scoring" (acquiring drugs). The group had social bonds based on kinship and very long-term friendship that helped to maintain the group, but the members never got together socially. One of our ethnographic respondents described the group's primary activity, "scoring":

> Somebody in the group will get ahold of the others when they want to score or when they are going to score. Whoever wants some will put their money together and someone will go to . . . (major city) . . . , usually and get the stuff and call the others. The others will come and get their part and go home and use.

These drug users tended to be very secretive. Most of them were married or in monogamous relationships. They were employed at various economic levels. They might use drugs on a maintenance level during the week and get "loaded" on weekends or special occasions. The major area of risk for HIV transmission was contact with people outside of their own group (**weak ties**) whose HIV status was unknown.

 Definition: Weak ties are links between people characterized by lack of intimacy and infrequent contact

These networks are quite different from *family-based networks*, which are predominantly kinship groups (parents; children; siblings; in-laws; or fictive kinship, godparenthood, or *compadrazgo* relationships in the Hispanic communities). One particular drug network we studied consisted of a three-generation family of more than 10 injection drug users. Members of this network were born into, had married into, or had a steady sexual partner in the group. The participants had gone to school together, and many were raised together. The groups tended to be homogeneous in terms of socioeconomic status and ethnic identification. Drug use with this group could be considered a family tradition; a special case of peer pressure. The individual faced very strong pressure to conform to group norms. The nonuser was considered to be condemning the group's behavior. An example of this was reported by a group member who was attempting to abstain from drug use:

> They called me names, they said I was too good for them. . . . I fought with them. . . . I beat two of them up, but I still had to go to the hospital.

HIV risk for this group primarily involved the sharing of injection equipment among family and friends. For the most part, these kinds of networks involved individuals in long-standing monogamous partnerships, and there was little exchange of sex for drugs, although in some of the partnerships, co-use of sex and drugs could be found. Any one of several drugs could have been the drug of choice for the group; the most common were cocaine, crack, rock, crystal meth, marijuana, and alcohol.

Long-term friendship networks (friendship-based networks) were semi-open systems whose members scored together and were socially bonded through drug use. The majority of these networks were relatively homogeneous in terms of socioeconomic status and ethnicity. They consisted of friends who were alike and who liked each other. The predominant social bonds in the group were long-term friendships, although some kinship relationships were usually present. Individuals in these networks involved one another in both drug use and in other types of social activities. The members often were connected through work. These groups were somewhat open to recruitment of new members, although recruitment took time. "Good friends" could be invited to "party" (use drugs) with the group, but it was very common for a group to take from 1 year to 18 months to get to know someone before he or she was recruited. Multiple drugs were used in this type of group, including heroin, cocaine, crack, speed, and alcohol. The groups also tended to include both injectors and noninjectors in the same network. A respondent described a night of mixed drug use as follows: "People will be drinking or doing coke, and those who want to shoot up go in the other room." Risk for this group centered on the sharing of works (drug paraphernalia, needles) "among friends." Sexual activity could also be present within the group, with multiple sexual partners a possibility and with changing sexual relationships within the group over time. Sex was sometimes exchanged for drugs, although this tended to involve ongoing social relationships rather than commercial transactions.

Convenience (acquaintance) networks are the most open of the four drug network types. They often included users of many kinds of drugs who "bridged," or skipped from group to group. The most common drug used was crack cocaine, and crack dealers tended to operate more openly than most of the other suppliers. Introduction into the group could be accelerated if an individual had become a known buyer. Acquaintances with little knowledge of the person would make the introduction to the group's dealer, saying "He's okay, he's buying." This indicated that the existing group member had seen and had been with the new person when the new person was scoring, or buying drugs. Having a known supply of money was an important credential for entry into these networks and expedited acceptance. Individuals in these groups regularly exchanged sex for drugs, and there were far more "impersonal" exchanges in them than in the other groups. A long-time drug user derogatorily referred to members of this type of group as "trash can addicts" because they would use any kind of drug. These networks tended to consist of users who were new in the area and looking for contacts, people who had progressed to a level of drug use that made them unattractive to members of the more closed groups, users in transition between groups, and young drug users who had not been recruited to a stable network. As a respondent indicated, "I was here chipping, running back and forth to [a nearby metropolitan area] for a year before I finally ran into one person, and from them I met about 10 others."

The convenience, or acquaintance groups appeared to be at highest risk for HIV infection because they engaged in a full range of activities involving the exchange of sex for drugs (commercial and noncommercial) and needle sharing with strangers. They also included a large proportion of individuals who were highly mobile and who were likely to move back and forth to nearby urban areas during the year, increasing local risks because of their contact with higher HIV prevalence sites.

➤●➤●➤

Knowing the types of networks and their associated HIV risk was valuable for our AIDS prevention project. It allowed us to relate drug users' social contexts to other types of behavior. We used statistical procedures to test the usefulness of the classification system and found that network membership was an important predictor of the likelihood of getting tested for HIV (an important element in preventing the disease). The networks also differed in the frequency of overall drug use among members, the context of drug use (family vs. friends vs. strangers), the frequency of injection (from not using injectable drugs to frequent injection and sharing needles), the frequency and type of sexual encounters within the networks, and the frequency of self-protection by using condoms. These kinds of data were very useful for targeting HIV intervention and education activities.

Interaction and "Embedded Behaviors"

Much research in the social sciences has concentrated on individual behavior, motivations, and other personal conditions that influence behavior. However, many human behaviors are not conducted alone. Most are the result of interactions, not simple reactions, and network research is preeminently the study of these interactions. Social network research is extremely important for examining specific kinds of behavior in the context of interaction, particularly in cases where researchers want to study if, how, and the conditions under which people do change their behavior. Such research takes place within the context where change in behavior is supposed to take place (i.e., in personal and social networks). The more that can be learned about how behaviors are embedded in a network context, the more likely we will be to make significant strides in understanding human behavior.

One example of the importance of studying embedded behaviors comes from research done on adolescents. Although individual teenagers can differ in their motivation, their intention to behave or misbehave, and their own values or norms, it is clear that, at least for most historically Euro-American cultures, the actual behavior of teenagers is much more likely to match that of their peers than that of any other group. Peer pressure occurs within a natural network, and studying how the structure and elements of a network condition individual behavior can tell us a great deal about how cultural systems, including those of teenagers, really work. For example, young people often start using drugs such as alcohol and marijuana because their friends offer such drugs to them and put pressure on the teens to use them. Doing so demonstrates that they "belong" to the group. By contrast, other teen peer groups can protect their members against such risks because members support each other in avoiding harmful behavior. These conditions can be studied through an ethnographic description of the behaviors associated with specific networks and the processes through which such behaviors are transferred and

 Key point supported or encouraged. *The advantage of ethnographic description is that it can discover behavioral details and patterns of communication and influence specific to the group, which can then be quantified when the ethnographer wishes to measure them in other networks.*

Cross-Group Differences

Ethnographic network research also is useful for comparing and contrasting differences in social groups as well as differences in group dynamics across cultural, social, age, and gender configurations. It also can be used to consider how the characteristics of networks influence behaviors (both positively and negatively) and meet social needs. For example, different kinds of kinship groups can be examined for the ways in which they affect people's behavior. The study of **voluntary associations** in various cultures provides another example of the economic, social, and spiritual impact that those associations have on individuals' survival and success across cultures.

Definition: Voluntary associations are those that people join voluntarily to meet a variety of their personal, economic, and social needs

---

Steps in the Conduct of Network Ethnography

- Identify "neighborhoods" or geographic areas where research will take place.
- Obtain lists of "groups" by name or local jargon/terminology from local experts in the research domain.
- Identify individuals who are members of these groups.
- Develop rapport—a close and trusting relationship with these individuals—by spending time with them in the field.
- Use interviewing and participant observation techniques to gather information about them, their group, their activities, and the relationships of group members.
- Interview as many other members of the group as possible to find out whether their views of the group, their activities, and their relationships are similar to each other. This helps to define inclusion/exclusion rules (the boundaries of the group), bridges, bonds, activities, and relationships with other groups.
- Continue this work with other named or otherwise identified groups.

■ Systematically compare and contrast groups on an ongoing basis (using continuous comparison) to identify dimensions or characteristics of difference in structures, boundaries, and behaviors among groups.

■ Use either qualitative or quantitative (survey) methods to associate network (group) characteristics with other behaviors of group members (e.g., drug or sex risk, educational achievement, social mobility).

EGO-CENTERED APPROACHES TO UNDERSTANDING NETWORKS

Personal or ego-centered networks form one of the main cultural conditions that determine positive or negative outcomes for peoples' lives. They are a primary cultural anchor point, as indicated by the Spanish proverb quoted at the beginning of the chapter. People resemble and are influenced in their behavior and belief by those with whom they associate. Information about ego-centered personal networks allows anthropologists to quickly establish some of the important traits of "average" or typical networks in a given culture. These traits, such as the size of networks, the closeness and duration of relationships between ego and personal network members, and the impact of peer norms on ego can be collected from each person or from a selected sample of people in a community or a culture.

Personal network data normally are collected as part of a larger survey, using either questionnaires that people fill out themselves or an interview where everyone is asked the same set of questions. Figure 1.1a provides examples of questions asked to interviewees (egos) about their networks (alters); Figure 1.1b is an example of a form that can be used to fill in basic information about alters.[1]

Figure 1.2 lists questions asked of egos about the drug and risk behavior of each alter.

You have listed _____ people that you identify as being important to you, or being significantly involved in your life in some way. For each one of these individuals, I would like you to answer the following questions *to the best of your ability.*

Q44. Is _____ male or female?
     Male   1
     Female   2

Q45. Is _____ (Interviewer: read list and circle *only* one):
     Black (not Hispanic)   1
     White (not Hispanic)   2
     Hispanic/Latino (ASK Q45a BELOW)   3
     Other (Specify): _____   4
     DK/Unsure   77
     Refused   88

     NOTE TO INTERVIEWER: FOR OTHER THAN HISPANIC, GO TO Q62 BELOW

Q45a. (If Hispanic, ASK) Is _____ (Interviewer: read list and circle *only* one):
     Puerto Rican   1
     Cuban   2
     Mexican Am./Chicano   3
     Mexican   4
     Dominican Republican   5
     Central or South American   6
       Specify country _____
     Other _____   7
     DK/Unsure   77
     Refused   88

Q46. How old is _____ ?
     AGE _____   DK/UNSURE—77   REFUSED—88

Q47. What is _____ 's relationship to you?

01 Mother/Father	07 Niece/Nephew	13 Lover, girls/boyfriend	19 Dealer
02 Sister/Brother	08 Grandchild	14 Ex-lover/Ex-spouse	20 Houseman
03 Child	09 Spouse	15 Friend	21 Doctor
04 Grandparent	10 Mo./Fa. In-law	16 Roommate	22 Counselor
05 Aunt/Uncle	11 Si./Br. In-law	17 Neighbor	23 Priest/Pastor/etc.
06 Cousin	12 Compadres/ Commadres	18 Running Buddy/ Associate	24 Other _____

Q48. How long have you known _____?

  Q48a.   Months _____   Q64b.   Years _____

Q49. On a scale of 1 (not at all) to 5 (extremely), how strong is your relationship with _____?
     (Score) _____   DK/UNSURE 7   REFUSED 8

Q50. On a scale of 1 (not at all) to 5 (extremely), how important is _____ to you?
     (Score) _____   DK/UNSURE 7   REFUSED 8

Q51. On a scale of 1 (not at all) to 5 (completely), how much can you trust _____?
     (Score) _____   DK/UNSURE 7   REFUSED 8

Q52. If you were HIV positive, or had AIDS, would you be willing to tell _____?
     No 0   Yes 1   DK/UNSURE 7   REFUSED 8

Q53. How many days in the past 30 days have you been in contact (in person, phone, etc.) with this person?
            Number of days _____

Figure 1.1a. Elicitation of background data on alters.

This instrument is an adaptation of a network questionnaire used by the Institute for Community Research and the Hispanic Health Council in Hartford, Connecticut to record information on individuals' alters or members of their social networks.

DATE: _____

PARTICIPANT ID#: _____   MASTER #: _____

#	Full and Nick Name(s)	Relationship	Sex m/f	Eth. aa/l/w/o	Age
1					
2					
3					
4					
5					
6					
7					
8					
9					
10					
11					
12					
13					
14					
15					
16					
17					
18					
19					
20					

Figure 1.1b. Basic data entry form for identification of alters.[1]

Data such as these can be recorded in a data collection matrix such as the one in Figure 1.3, and then used in conjunction with questions such as those listed above in Figure 1.1a.

To use the social networks matrix give each alter a number from 1 to 25. That number is used in the data matrix to refer to the alter. Question numbers head each column of the matrix, and the questionnaire is physically placed beside the matrix during the interview. As the questions are asked,

HIV RISK BEHAVIORS: NETWORK MEMBERS

	No	Yes	DK/Unsure	Refused
Q54. Does _____ know that you use drugs?	No 0	Yes 1	DK/Unsure 7	Refused 8
Q55. Does _____ provide you with drugs of any kind?	No 0	Yes 1	DK/Unsure 7	Refused 8
Q56. Do you provide _____ with drugs of any kind?	No 0	Yes 1	DK/Unsure 7	Refused 8
Q57. Does _____ inject drugs?	No 0	Yes 1	DK/Unsure 7	Refused 8
Q58. Does _____ inject drugs in a shooting gallery?	No 0	Yes 1	DK/Unsure 7	Refused 8
Q59. Does _____ inject drugs, using needles that he/she knows had been used by someone else?	No 0	Yes 1	DK/Unsure 7	Refused 8
Q60. Does _____ share needles in a shooting gallery?	No 0	Yes 1	DK/Unsure 7	Refused 8
Q61. Does _____ inject drugs using needles that had previously been used by you?	No 0	Yes 1	DK/Unsure 7	Refused 8
Q62. Do you inject drugs using needles that had previously been used by _____?	No 0	Yes 1	DK/Unsure 7	Refused 8
Q63. Does _____ share cookers or cotton with other people?	No 0	Yes 1	DK/Unsure 7	Refused 8
Q64. Do you and _____ share cookers or cotton?	No 0	Yes 1	DK/Unsure 7	Refused 8

Figure 1.2. Drug risk behavior of alters.
This instrument is an adaptation of a network questionnaire used by the Institute for Community Research and the Hispanic Health Council in Hartford, Connecticut to record information on HIV-related risk of the individuals' alters or members of their social networks.

the matrix is filled in with codes corresponding to the informant's answers.

To assess the connectedness of the network, from ego's perspective, respondents may be asked how each member of the personal network interacts with every other member —based on their own knowledge (see Figure 1.4). Later in this chapter, we will discuss how a full relational network analysis proceeds from this point.

PARTICIPANT ID#: _____

MASTER #: _____   DATE: _____

[INTERVIEWER: Refer to Social Network Interview Guide for questions to fill out matrix. Copy list of network members by full and nick names and general characteristics on Network Matrix Pull Out List.]

#	Initials	43a Drugs with	43b Inj with	43c Sex with	43d Close with	43e Confl with	44 M/F	45 Ethn.	45a Hisp Eth.	46 Age	47 Relat. Code	48a Memb. know	48b Yrs. know	49 Strength relat.	50 Import. relat.	51 Treat relat.	52 Tell HIV+	53 Days contact	54 Know use dr	55 Provide you dr	56 You prov. dr	57 Inj. drugs	58 Inj. in gallery	59 You used needles	60 Share ndl. gall	61 Use you/U used ndl	62 U use X's used ndl	63 X share condom	64 U & X share cdm
1																													
2																													
3																													
4																													
5																													
6																													
7																													
8																													
9																													
10																													
11																													
12																													
13																													
14																													
15																													
16																													

Total network members: _____

---

[2] This instrument is an adaptation of a data collection matrix used by the Institute for Community Research and the Hispanic Health Council in Hartford, Connecticut, to record basic demographic and drug risk related data from "ego" about the members of his or her social network ("alters")..

Figure 1.3. Social Network Matrix

Figure 1.4. Data recording matrix for collection of data on interaction of all members of the network.

TABLE 1.1   Gender, Age, and Ethnic Distribution of Respondents, and Respondent's
            30-Day and Recent Use Networks

	Respondent (Ego)[a]	People in Respondent's 30-Day Network[b]	Alters Present in Most Recent Use[c]
Gender			
Male	34 (67)[d]	81 (63)	62 (68)
Female	18 (33)	46 (37)	28 (31)
Age			
10-19[e]	12 (23)	36 (28)	28 (31)
20-29	14 (26)	38 (29)	25 (27)
30-39	23 (44)	43 (33)	30 (33)
40-49	3 (5)	9 (7)	7 (7)
50-59	0 (0)	1 (1)	0 (0)
Ethnicity			
African American	10 (19)	22 (17)	16 (17)
Hispanic	19 (36)	64 (50)	42 (46)
Anglo	18 (34)	35 (27)	27 (30)
Native American	5 (9)	6 (4)	5 (5)

a. N = 52.
b. N = 127.
c. N = 90.
d. The number in brackets is the percentage figure.
e. In order to participate, individuals had to be 18 years of age or older, could not have been in
treatment in the past 12 months, and had to have a positive urine screen for cocaine or heroine,
or needle marks (tracks) and a positive urine screen for some other injectable illicit drug.
Therefore, this category includes only 18- and 19-year-olds.

Information such as that collected in Figures 1.1 – 1.4,
which is used to describe typical personal networks, is
normally reported in the form of tables such as the one
above, which comes from the Flagstaff Multicultural AIDS
Prevention Project (FMAPP). Table 1.1 compares the people who provided the information (respondents or ego)
with the people whom they named as being part of their
personal network (alters). In this case, we asked about the
demographic characteristics of people who were part of
their network for the past 30 days, and people who were
present the last time they used drugs with other people.

When we analyzed all of the personal network questions
in our questionnaire, we found that the number of people

with whom each respondent (ego) reported spending time ranged from 0 (they were isolated) to more than 25 people, with the majority responding that they spent time with from 1 to 10 other people. Thus, the typical personal network included up to 10 family members (all but 16 of the respondents fell into this range). These relatively small networks commonly include both users and nonusers, some kin relations, and close friends. Only 25% responded that all of the people with whom they spent time use drugs. Of those alters who used drugs, 25% injected drugs, 69% smoked crack, and the rest used some other drug.

By combining and examining all of the ego-centered network data, we determined that the majority of drug networks are small (2 to 10 individuals), are based on close friendships or kinship ties, and are relatively stable in their composition. The data also indicated that the majority of risky encounters, such as needle-sharing activities or sexual relationships, occur with the first three people named by ego as members of his or her network. A smaller proportion of the needle-sharing and sexual encounters occur with people outside of ego's close personal network, but the data also indicate that it is exactly these encounters, called weak ties, that are the most risky kinds of contacts for the majority of drug users. Weak ties are defined by less intimacy and infrequent association. Based on these data, part of our HIV prevention and education effort has been directed at making recommendations that would help these individuals break, reduce, or decrease the risks associated with their weak-tie relationships.

In the same project, we also explored how useful other ego-centered measures of network structure were in identifying conditions that linked individual social networks to the individual's risk of spending time in jail or becoming infected with HIV through drug use. This process allowed us to use relatively simple and nonthreatening questions that could be asked about individuals' social relationships,

Definition: Ties are links between people that are measured by perceived intimacy and frequency of association. Indicators of tie strength are "How close are you to X?" and "How often do you see X?"

yet it also told us important information about their probable health status and risk-taking behavior.

EXAMPLE 1.1　　　　　　　　　◆━●━◆━●━◆

THE NATURE OF RISKS IN PERSONAL NETWORKS

In our study of drug use and its relationship to HIV/AIDS risk, we were able to collect data from a total of 496 active drug users. We hypothesized that the nature of personal relationships (close to distant, dense to dispersed, and few to multiple connections among members) had an impact on the average level of risk that a person incurs over time. Measuring different elements of personal network structure should show a significant relationship to the HIV, drug, and incarceration risks of individuals. This is possible because differences in personal networks may result in differences in the amount of information that passes to a particular individual, the length of time it takes information to reach a person in the network, differences in people who are gatekeepers for the information flow, measures of differential influence in the group, and measures of the probability that someone can or cannot receive information sent through the network (cf. Doreian, 1974; Ford & Fulkerson, 1956; Gomory & Hu, 1964; Katz, 1953; Taylor, 1969).

We assumed that risk taking is a generalized, rather than specific, activity for individuals. If they take risks in one area of their life, they are much more likely to take risks in other areas. Therefore, the individuals who are most likely to accept early recruitment into our program are more likely to be higher risk takers than are the individuals recruited from the same network later in the process. Because they do not know us or our project well, it is as much a risk for them to participate (and possibly be caught up in a drug sting) as it is for them to interact with other strangers. We felt that coming into the project as one of the first members of a network to be recruited (i.e., acting as bridging individuals) might be a proxy measure for individual influence or centrality in the network. We based our analysis on the assumption that the individuals most willing to try out a new program were also those most likely to take the lead in other social undertakings, or risky behavior.

We were able to show that the program recruitment order data (the rank order in which each individual was recruited into the project for their network) not only correlated with network structure measures (how they were connected, what subgroup they belonged to, etc.), but also were related to increased risk taking (Trotter, Bowen, Baldwin, & Price, 1996; Trotter, Bowen, & Potter, 1995; Trotter, Potter, Bowen, & Jiron, 1994). Early arrivals in each network were more likely to have tried a drug treatment program than were the later recruits in the same network, whereas later arrivals were more likely to have no injection-drug-user sex partners. Those recruited earlier in networks were very likely to have sex partners who were also injection drug users—that is, they participated in double-risk relationships.

We also hypothesized that participation in two or more networks involved more potential risk and risk taking than did membership in a single network. Three hundred twenty-one individuals in our study participated in only one drug network (66.5%), and 162 individuals (33.5%) were members of two or more drug networks. Analysis confirmed this hypothesis. We were thus able to conclude that simply asking individuals to self-identify as having either single or multiple network membership was sufficient to provide a direct indication of both their type and level of risk taking in their personal drug-using networks.

➤•➤•➤

These results showed us that this type of personal or ego-centered network data collection could be very useful for finding out important facts about the most common personal networks of individuals in our projects. The same type of information could be easily collected on personal networks associated with participation in educational or economic development programs, social integration into community life, exposure to violence, gang affiliation, or any other cultural domain.

*Steps in the Collection and Analysis
of Ego-Centered Network Data*

- Develop an instrument on your topic that includes collection of information on the research topic (e.g., drug use) in five ways:
  1. From the individual
  2. About each individual (alter) mentioned by the individual
  3. About the interaction of the individual with each alter
  4. Whether alters know each other
  5. What known risk behaviors occur between each alter and all others
- Identify a representative sample of individuals (or include these questions in your regular survey)
- Interview the sample of individuals

In the following box, we describe the steps used to analyze ego-centered network data in a study of drug use. In this study, the network characteristics of ego with regard to risky drug- and sex-related behavior can be analyzed in association with other behaviors or conditions, such as whether ego and his or her alters are infected with the HIV virus. Demographic and other known risk-related differences in the characteristic of ego-centered networks can be identified and the origins and impact of those differences explored. In the example below, these network differences include size of network, gender ratio, and drug risk indexes. Ethnographers can use the procedures similar to those listed in the box for network studies addressing any other topic in the social sciences.

An Example of the Steps in Analyzing Egocentric Network Data

1. Describe the networks of individuals in terms of the following:

   - Network size
   - Gender ratio
   - Sexual preference
   - Ethnicity ratio (the relative proportions of people from various ethnic groups)
   - Age (in terms of the mean and modal age of members, the range of ages in the network, and their standard deviation)
   - Ratio of kin to nonkin sexual partners among members
   - Intensity of the relationships between ego and all other members of the network[2]

2. Establish levels of risk for ego as an individual by creating two indexes: a drug risk index and a sex risk index.

   - Sum up all of ego's risky drug behaviors.
   - Sum up all of ego's risky sex behaviors.
   - Add together the sum of ego's risky drug behaviors and the sum of ego's risky sex behaviors.
   - This sum total is an overall index of risk behavior for an individual.

3. Establish risk indexes for drugs and sex (as above in #2) for every network contact based on what ego reports for the contact or alter.

4. Obtain ego's total risk exposure score using the following steps:

   - Add ego's combined drug and sex risk index to the combined drug and sex risk indexes for all network members (obtained in #3 above)
   - Divide this total score by the number of people in ego's network to create an average risk index

5. Obtain the total risk exposure score of ego's network.

   - Count and add together risky behaviors of all alters with one another

Definition:
Connected-
ness is the extent
of reciprocal
relationships
among individuals
in a network

 Definition:
Power/
influence is the
degree to which a
person in a network
gives and receives
information or
other resources

 Definition:
Role
relationships
are those associated
with a particular
place or position
in a social network

 Definition:
Cliques/
components
are subunits within a
larger network
designated by the
greater strength of
their interconnected-
ness compared with
other parts of the
network

 Definition:
Density is the
actual number
of relationships
found in a network
compared to the
total number of
possible relationships

The variables obtained in this way measure variations in ego-centered networks that differ from variation created by demographic characteristics. They can be correlated with demographic variables and used as "predictors" or correlates of other behavior or conditions (such as health or mental health status).

FULL NETWORK RELATIONSHIPS: RECIPROCAL NETWORK INFORMATION

Data collected about the reciprocal relationships within social networks can be very useful in helping ethnographers understand complex conditions in everyday life. Ethnographic research on entire relational networks includes information about **connectedness**; the **power and influence** that individual actors exhibit in a network; the **role relationships** that are demonstrated in a network; the impact of that particular social network position (such as a bridge, or a particular configuration of network connections) on people; the subdivision of the network into **cliques and components**; and the overall **density** of a given network, compared with other networks. The following sections identify some of the most common ways that these aspects of networks are analyzed and understood.

Communication Flow

Communication (speaking, visiting, sending messages) in networks can be assessed by measuring the presence or absence of changes in the level of information flow within the network (Hubbell, 1965; Taylor, 1969). Network data can be collected to identify the presence or absence of particular topics or of communication between individuals and between sets of individuals. The patterns of information flow within networks, sometimes called *connectivity* (Doreian, 1974), can be characterized by several measures, including the amount of information that passes through a network, identification of the people who are gatekeepers to the information flow, measures of differential influence in the group, and measures of the probability that someone can or cannot receive information that is introduced into the network (Ford & Fulkerson, 1956; Gomory & Hu, 1964; Katz, 1953; Taylor, 1969). A social network research project that focused on communication would describe most or all of these conditions for each of the relationships or behaviors that were studied.

Distance and Segmentation

Network researchers have created two primary methods for identifying key structural elements of groups. One is based on the idea of social cohesion, where cliques or circles of social actors are identified by the bonds that link them together (Bron & Kerbosch, 1973; Mokken, 1979). The other is based on the idea of structural equivalence, where people who are similarly connected (have the same types of links to others) are thought to be more similar to each other than to people in the same network who have different types of links to others (Burt, 1976; Kilworth & Bernard, 1974). These different measures all provide information on the ways that networks work.

Some of the configurations of relationships and the changes in relationships between individuals in a network also can be identified. Changes may be caused by some kind of intervention or event, or they may be attributable to natural changes in people's lives. These changes can be assessed by the number of reduced connections among all network members or among some portions of the network (Burt, 1976; Doreian, 1974), or by looking at changes in the composition or location of subgroups or cliques and the reasons for them. For example, in some of our drug-using networks, people who go into drug treatment programs decide not to interact with their drug-using friends in order to stay away from drugs. This avoidance causes significant changes in the social networks of both the drug users and the nonusers.

Positions and Roles of Network Members

The roles people play and the positions they hold in a network also affect how communication flows in a network, because people who are more central to a network tend to have control over information. Looking at the centralization of a network provides a way to measure the degree to which information is controlled by specific individuals within a network (Stephenson & Zelen, 1991). For some networks, a reduction of centralization should correlate with the creation of more communication linkages between noncentral individuals. Careful ethnographic observation should be able to detect changes in influence, as is the case when individuals take on new roles within the group (Bonacich, 1987). Ethnographic studies should also be able to detect changes in influence, both for drug taking and sexual issues, as individuals take on new roles within the group to reinforce protective behaviors and reduce risks. These issues are explored below with examples from an instrument used in one of our Flagstaff projects to illustrate how data can be collected on these characteristics.

EXAMPLE 1.2   ━◆━●━◆●━

FULL RELATIONSHIP DATA FOR DRUG USER NETWORKS

One of our substance abuse projects provided full network relationship data on a total of 10 active drug-using networks. The size of these groups varied from 5 to 42 people. During the full network data collection process, we brought each group together and asked the members to rate their interactions with each member of their network based on a structured set of questions about their social relationships, their drug use patterns, and communication about intimate subjects such as sex (see Figure 1.5).

TRUST

T1 How honest is _____ with you?

T2 How often does _____ tell important things to you?

T3 How comfortable would _____ be to share works with you?

T4 How often does _____ tell his/her problems to you?

T5 If you had AIDS, how willing would you be to tell _____?

SOCIAL relationship measures

S1 How much do you hang around with _____?

S2 How close a friend is _____?

DRUG relationship measures

D1 How often do you use drugs with _____?

D2 How often do you go to _____ for drugs?

Combined INTIMACY/TRUST measures

I1 How comfortable would you feel discussing AIDS with _____?

I2 How comfortable would you feel discussing an affair with _____?

I3 How comfortable would you feel discussing unwanted sex with _____?

Figure 1.5. Full relational network data collection instrument.

Analysis of this relational network data allowed us to describe each of these groups according to the conventional types of analysis that can be run on network relational data (cf. Burt, 1976; Glover 1989, 1990; Kilworth & Bernard, 1974; Knoke & Kuklinski, 1983; Panning, 1982; Scott 1991). A description of one of these networks illustrates the types of information we were able to gather by this method (Trotter, Bowen, & Potter, 1995; Trotter et al., 1996; Trotter, Rothenberg, & Coyle, 1995). This network is a multigeneration, family-based, drug-using network. It contains members from two kinship groups. The group includes both males and females who are drug users. The drugs of choice for the group are cocaine and crystal meth (methamphetamine), and the group includes both injection drug users and noninjection drug users. The socioeconomic status of the group is low, as denoted by the fact that they live in local public housing projects and receive welfare, or government-provided financial assistance. Three individuals from Mexico who do not have legal residency documents for the United States are members of the group. The core group has been using drugs together since high school, with some of the members now in their 40s. The network is relatively closed; membership is restricted to kin and sexual partners of kin.

The relationships in this network can be thought of as

- The different types of connections between **actors**—the common network term used for identifying different individuals in the network
- The centrality or influence of individual actors, or of subgroups within the larger group
- Roles or "positions" that actors hold within the network (cf. Knoke & Kuklinski, 1982)

Relational network information is commonly presented in the form of diagrams, charts, tables, data matrices, cluster diagrams, and verbal descriptions.[3] One of the most common ways of displaying the data is to construct a sociogram that indicates actors by circles, and connections or interactions among them by lines. The diagram on the following page (Figure 1.6) is a model of the social relationships in the drug-using network.

The connecting lines between individuals (identified by a number) indicate the existence of a strong connection between those two people. All individuals in this group have some weak interactions with each other, but the influence or communication between some is minimal; Figure 1.6 concentrates on the strong ties. Females are represented by a number in a circle, and males by a number in a square. An arrowhead indicates a one-way connection between two people, whereas a solid line indicates a two-way connection. The width of the line indicates the strength of the connection. For example, the larger, shaded circle around Anita,[4] #13, indicates that she is the central person in terms of influence measures. She is also the most central communication node in the network. The core of the network is composed of Anita (#13), Lydia (#6), Adelita (#4), Marcos (#5), Jaime (#9), and Josepha (#3). All of these individuals have close kinship ties, and communication among them is strong (i.e., frequent and intimate). Miguel (#11) and Dolores (#12) are married, and Miguel is the first cousin of

Figure 1.6. Social relations diagram.

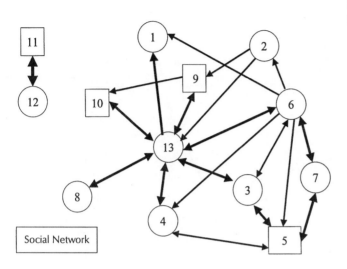

Maria (#1) and Lydia (#6). Aida (#7) is Lydia's (#6) niece and Josepha's (#3) first cousin.

The *drug network* characteristics, which we derived from analysis of the drug questions on our network matrix, are an interesting contrast to the *social* relationships described previously. In the drug-related networks, several people changed position from peripheral to more strongly connected, or vice versa, as can be seen in Figure 1.7 below.

Drug issues create a change in the information flow and influence patterns of the network. Aida (#7) is a nonuser, which is clearly represented in her lack of connections on the drug questions. Anita (#13) shares the influence in drug networks with her son, Marcos (#5), and with Jaime (#9), who is a central member because he is a bilingual communication bridge between the Spanish (only) and the English (only) portions of the network. Marcos (#5) scores drugs for this network, keeps track of drug-related conditions, and

Figure 1.7. Drug
relations diagram.

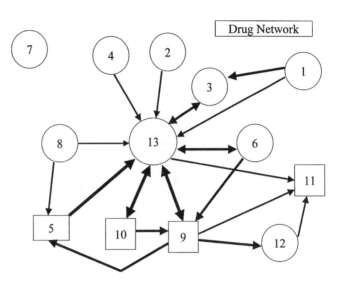

influences the network through his mother's close connections with everyone else. Some of the individuals who were
strongly connected by social relationships are connected by
weak ties, or no longer directly connected in terms of their
drug relations. For example, #4 and #5, who are married to
each other, are strongly tied in the diagram on social relationships, but #4 does not communicate much about drugs
with her husband, only with her mother-in-law (#13). The
kinship ties between #9 and #2 (living as married) are not
visible in the drug relationship diagram, nor is the aunt-
niece connection between #6 and #7. This indicates that
some people who can be reached for *drug-related* HIV risk
reduction information through the drug relationships network must be accessed via different people and lines of
communication if they are to receive *social* risk reduction
information, such as information about the need to reduce
the number of sexual risks they encounter or how to nego-
tiate condom use.

We have also analyzed several other classic measures of network connections and network structure[5] for this group of drug users. An analysis of the network structures termed **factions and cliques** associated with the drug use network (cf. Borgatti, Everett, & Shirey, 1990; Bron & Kerbosch, 1973; Seidman & Foster, 1978) indicates that when social relations alone are considered, most members are closely connected to central members; only a small number of people are marginal to the core of the group (Figure 1.6). However, the configuration within the group changes significantly when the drug relation questions are analyzed. In this second analysis, the core drug group is divided into two subsystems: a predominantly English-speaking clique, and a predominantly Spanish-speaking clique. This division was discovered in our initial ethnographic research and confirmed in this second, quantitative analysis.

This information on cliques and factions can be used to identify boundaries where information needed for the successful implementation of an intervention may be blocked unless at least one individual from each subgroup is involved in the intervention. Information provided to centralized networks like this one, which has only a few marginal individuals, passes through fewer contacts and through a smaller number of individuals than it does in diffuse, less tightly constructed networks. Moreover, if a network is badly fissured or fragmented, information must be provided to multiple individuals.

As a final note on the relationships displayed by these two representations, the shape of the drug relations network diagram (Figure 1.7) is very similar to a classic problem-solving configuration displayed by networks. It is called a star pattern; in it one person acts as a center who is in direct communication with the rest of the network through dyadic relationships and who has relatively few interconnections among other members of the network. This configuration allows rapid input from the central

Definition:
Factions and cliques are small groups formed by their close and special connections to one another within a larger network

person to all members on any issue, thus facilitating problem solving for the group as a whole. The social network diagram (Figure 1.7) is a classic communication configuration where there are **multiplex ties** within the group. Multiplex ties mean that each individual has several different kinds of relationships with the other people in the group at the same time. This structure ensures that loss of a network member will not cause communication to break down, because everyone in the core group is tied to a number of other people and connected to each other through many different relationships.

These findings parallel those from other networks we have investigated. The majority of drug-using networks are small and relatively tight. They depend on kinship and long-term friendship for entry, and they show a strong tendency for tight communication and reinforcement of the group's norms. These norms can support the elimination of risks through the elimination of ties that produce HIV risks, such as needle sharing with strangers or unprotected sex with casual partners. In addition, the existing boundaries can be reinforced, and some assessment of HIV risk can be added to the trust issues that already affect new recruitment in the group. New recruits could be sought only from among people who engage in low-risk categories of drug abuse or sexual behavior. All of this information allows us to go far beyond an understanding of individual network members into the social organization and culture of drug use and relevant associated social action.

Definition: Multiplex ties in a group means that each group member has many different relationships with most or all other members in a group

NETWORK SAMPLING STRATEGIES

Cross Reference: Sampling strategies are discussed in Books 1 and 2 and Chapter 3 of this Book

Ego-centered network sampling is based on random, representative, or any other form of quota sampling. Full relational network sampling begins with the identification of individuals who act as entry points to the network. Entry to a full relational network can begin with any specific individual in the network. Usually, however, there are multiple entry points. Once the ethnographer has identified people who can grant entry to the network, the next step in relational network sampling requires creating a sample using one of the following four different strategies:

- A complete sample of all individuals in the full network, or the entire population of the network
- A randomized sample of index individuals' alters
- Individuals screened and selected as index people because of their specific characteristics
- Individuals selected because they are the alters of a specific index person

Creating a Sample of All Individuals in the Full Network

This type of sampling is time-consuming and costly if the network is large and widely distributed, as it often is in an urban community. It is most useful when conducting research in smaller, bounded communities, such as classrooms, very small villages, girls' basketball teams, or circles of artisans and craftworkers.

Creating a Sample by Selecting a Randomized Sample of Index Individuals' Alters

To use this type of sample, the ethnographer first selects a number of index individuals for interviewing. If 10 index people are selected, they may, for example, identify up to 25 contacts or alters. From these 25 contacts, any number of individuals are then randomly selected for the second step of the interviewing process. For example, the ethnographer might randomly choose 6 people from the 25 identified alters for the second stage of the interview process. The ethnographer bases his or her decision regarding how many alters to interview on how many people are needed for the entire interview project.

During the second stage of interviews, each of the six alters is, in turn, asked to identify his or her own alters. The ethnographer then randomly selects six more alters of each of these six individuals for the third step of the interviewing process. Usually, only two to four "nodes," or interview steps —and consequent identification of people to interview— are feasible in a relational network study. More steps or nodes render the sample larger than needed.

Creating a Sample by Screening and Selecting Individuals Because of Their Special Characteristics

Often, social scientists seek to study individuals because they display the characteristics important for the study. For example, drug use studies might seek to find injection drug users; studies of campus politics would look for school leaders; health care studies would try to identify users of spiritual healers, or pregnant older women; ecological studies would seek environmental activists. These individuals are asked to list alters, and among alters, only those who fulfill specific criteria (such as those criteria used for identifying the specific individuals sought for the first step of interviews) are included in the sampling frame for the network sample. Thus, instead of selecting 6 alters randomly from a total of 25, 6 alters are selected on a randomized basis only from among those who possess or display the characteristics that are key to the study. Interviewing of index individuals continues on the same basis as above, organizing from two to four steps or nodes out to complete the desired sample size for the study.

Creating a Sample by Choosing an
Index Person and Selecting From
Among All of That Person's Alters

This type of sampling is called a "random walk design." It involves first selecting an index person and asking him or her to identify all of his or her alters. The next step involves randomly selecting one or more of these alters for interviewing. These alters, in turn, list their own alters. From these lists, the ethnographer randomly chooses one or more individuals to interview. In this way, the ethnographer can "walk" from linkage to linkage in a connected chain of individuals who are part of a much larger social network. The result is a randomized sample of the larger network structure.

SUMMARY AND CONCLUSIONS

A multiple method network approach has numerous advantages in an ethnographic research project. Ethnographic network mapping is fully compatible with other forms of ethnographic research. It can be accomplished best by a combination of observation and interviewing, and either of those approaches can be combined with other forms (or foci) of ethnographic data collection. It is possible to collect network data using a life history perspective, a cultural modeling approach, or reflexive and systematic cognitive methods. Because ego-centered networks represent components and entry points into larger network configurations, ego-centered data collection can form an interesting bridge to full reciprocal network data collection.

Once the basic norms, beliefs, and values of specific social groups have been discovered through the ethnographic approach, many anthropologists find that they need to turn to survey types of data collection. These efforts include household surveys, population-based (probabilistic) surveys, and special group questionnaires. It is

Cross Reference: See Books 2 and 3 for elicitation methods easy, and usually highly productive, to include ego-centered network questions along with the other questions embedded in this type of questionnaire. Of course, one must keep in mind that the addition of network questions takes quite a lot of extra time, so the purposes for including these questions must be defined clearly in your study.

Finally, full relational network data collection on reciprocal relationships in the network provides a level of detail about human groups that cannot be collected in any other manner. The overall measures of network structure and network connections that can be computed from network relational data are clearly associated with cultural differences in individual behavior. This approach shows a great deal of promise for both research and intervention work. Wherever data on the overall structures of full networks can be collected, these data can provide important guidelines for targeting both general (to everybody through social diffusion) and specific (to individuals) messages, and for developing community intervention programs, behavioral change training, and group assessment strategies.

Advantages of Ethnographic
Network Approaches

Advantages of Ethnographic Network Approaches

- Identifying and assessing hidden populations
- Recruiting, retaining, and following up on intervention populations
- Understanding personal social influences on the lives, decisions, and behaviors of individuals
- Enhancing the efficacy of behavioral interventions by working with groups that have maximum impact on the lives of the individuals who are members
- Understanding and intervening to change barriers and facilitators to information flow in order to reach individuals and groups more effectively

Many public health projects in the United States require making contacts with hard-to-reach or hidden populations, such as people who are asymptomatic carriers of infectious or genetically transmitted diseases, or people with socially or culturally stigmatized conditions, such as women who become pregnant without being married, homosexuals, or individuals who are infected with the HIV virus. This is a difficult process, and the hardest part of the outreach process is orchestrating initial entry into a new group that needs to be recruited for participation. Network-based outreach can make that recruitment easier because it follows existing social relationships, and once the initial contact is made, members of the network can recruit other members, rather than each new recruit requiring a cold contact from an outsider. This type of sponsorship process allows the network to control recruitment and to feel more comfortable about risking contact with strangers. The normal network gatekeepers can then act as go-betweens who reduce barriers to participation by endorsing the project to others in the network, rather than create barriers to participation.

Used in this way, network-based outreach can help establish the contacts and relationships necessary to conduct efficacious programs. It allows individuals to participate in intervention programs within the cultural context of a social group that will reinforce (or oppose) program objectives. A network approach is also extremely useful for keeping people in a program, or bringing them back in if they have dropped out. Most intervention programs that focus on individuals must rely on individualized motivational techniques. *Network methods are especially effective for* **Key point** *interventions because naturally existing network connections encourage participation and provide peer pressures that can reduce barriers to prevention and education and enhance retention.*

Network-based research programs have some additional advantages. Keeping track of network members is something the members of a network do naturally. This fact can assist in the long-term follow-up phase of any project, from ethnography to longitudinal survey research. If the core or most influential members of the network are identified and tracked, they can act as primary links between outreach workers and other members of the group. Because those core members—or gatekeepers—generally know the whereabouts of network members, they can make it easier for outreach workers—who usually have little time to track down and locate network members—to conduct individually based follow-up.

Our approach to risk reduction in small-town drug networks has proven to be valuable in the identification, location, and recruitment of hidden or difficult-to-access populations. Our ethnographic network analysis has led to a series of suggestions about combining qualitative and quantitative approaches in ways that increase our knowledge about HIV and drug intervention in "out-of-treatment" drug users. At the simplest level, network data identify the presence or absence of communication between individuals, and between sets of individuals, on particular topics. At the next level, network information data can identify the central person or people who exert the most influence on the group, the nodes (or central people) in the network who act as gatekeepers for interaction, or the subsets of individuals who interact more among themselves than they do with others in the larger network. Information on each of these factors can suggest plans for direct and indirect action and provide outcome measures of the efficacy of programs. Our data also explain the frequent failure of the classic strategy used in drug rehabilitation, health risk reduction, and most other public health interventions: moving an individual away from high-risk personal social networks into lower-risk relationships. Small-town drug networks are frequently kinship based, or based on long-term friendship. There are relatively few choices for making friends in a small town. There is a restricted pool from which to choose compared with an urban area with more groups and associations. In a small town, it is unfortunate if you do not like someone in your Narcotics Anonymous group, because it is the only one in town. People might have to leave town or even leave the state to accomplish the classic goal of changing friends and networks. Our data show that this is an unlikely or impossible event for most of the people we have interviewed. On the other hand, our network data indicate that it is possible to change the norms and risk-taking patterns of networks as a whole by reinforcing positive risk reduction behaviors. For this reason, natural network-based approaches to risk reduction are highly desirable adjuncts to individual intervention strategies.

These findings can be expanded to match up with other applied ethnographic programs and theories. Although they were designed within the context of medical anthropology, they can be transferred easily into any other area of culture in which groups have an impact on individual behavior. The three network approaches described in this chapter provide analytical tools that allow ethnographers to design and measure both the individual and the cumulative group effects of economic, agricultural, educational, ecological, political, and policy-oriented programs.

Our ethnographic findings demonstrate that we can use qualitative descriptions of network conditions as a direct adjunct to one type of applied program, and by extension to others. The ethnographic data act as an important theory-generating bridge to quantitative measures of the impact of social networks on cultural dynamics.

Researchers can measure both individual effects and cumulative network effects of any other type of applied programs or intervention using quantitative network data collection and analysis tools. The conditions that require increased communication can be measured by increased information flow within the network (Hubbell, 1965; Taylor, 1969). They are also measurable in terms of reduced distances among all network members, or some portions of the network (Burt, 1976; Doreian, 1974). For example, we learned from our HIV project that the size of the network probably affects the ease or the difficulty of changing group norms in ways that would protect members from risks in the community. It is probably harder to have an impact on larger, diffuse networks than on smaller, highly connected ones. We can measure differences in the overall risk to individuals and to the group as a whole based on the ratio of kin to nonkin membership, or the ratio of strong to weak ties, or on the basis of group norms that favor or interfere with positive attitudes toward drug treatment programs. Knowing the network membership of our participants allows us to measure peer influence on attempts to enter, or avoid, drug rehabilitation programs. We may be able to identify risk reduction in the network before and after high-risk elements of the network have been isolated or segmented off, and interactions with those cliques reduced or eliminated (Glover, 1989, 1990). We believe that factions within the network should show either risk reduction or risk increase, depending on their distance from the more risky elements or members of the network.

Centralization is a measure of the way that information is being controlled by individuals (Stephenson & Zelen, 1991), and for some networks, a reduction of centralization should correlate with risk reduction through the creation of more communication linkages between noncentral individuals. We also should be able to detect changes in influence, both in drug and socially related issues, when individuals take on new roles within the group to reinforce protective behaviors and reduce risks (Bonacich, 1987). We have also hypothesized that network relational and structural analysis can identify individuals who should become key players in network-level intervention and outreach, as adjuncts to project staff for a particular network.

An individual's potential for social, marital, economic, educational, or any other kind of success may be directly related to network variables. We should be able to measure the impact on individuals of such network characteristics, including such factors as divisions or conflicts in the group. We also should be able to assess differences in how groups within the networks address risk taking and how these differences affect the likelihood that both individuals and the groups will encounter risks. We may be able to detect changes in influence patterns when individuals assume new roles within the group that involve taking responsibility for encouraging group members to engage in protective behaviors and to reduce risks. In sum, network analysis in its various forms appears to be a highly desirable and productive tool for a wide variety of ethnographic research projects.

NOTES

1. Figures 1.1a, 1.1b, 1.2, 1.3, and 1.4 are taken from instruments currently in use for joint studies by the Institute for Community Research and the Hispanic Health Council on networks related to drug use and HIV risk, funded by the National Institute on Drug Abuse.

2. Intensity, as we explain later, is usually measured in terms of how often the ego sees a particular individual.

3. Full relational network data can be readily analyzed and displayed in a variety of diagram formats using two computerized programs developed by Borgatti and colleagues—UCINET and KRACKPLOT. These program resources are described as suggested resources at the end of this chapter.

4. All of the names in this description are pseudonyms to protect the identity of the individuals in the network. The networks we investigated included African Americans, Native Americans, Hispanics, and Anglo Americans. In this case, the example is a predominantly Hispanic network, but it easily could have been from any of the other cultural groups.

5. All of the calculations were conducted using the program UCINET 4.0 (Borgatti, 1993).

REFERENCES

Bonacich, P. (1987). Power and centrality: A family of measures. *American Journal of Sociology, 92,* 1170-1182.

Borgatti, S. P. (1993). *UCINET IV reference manual.* Columbia, SC: Analytic Technologies.

Borgatti, S. P., Everett, M. G., & Shirey, P. R. (1990). LS sets, lambda sets, and other cohesive subsets. *Social Networks, 12,* 337-357.

Bott, E. (1971). *Family and social network: Roles, norms, and external relationships in ordinary urban families.* London: Tavistock.

Bron, C., & Kerbosch, J. (1973). Finding all cliques of an undirected graph. *Comm of the ACM, 16,* 575-577.

Burt, R. (1976). Positions in networks. *Social Forces, 55,* 93-122.

Doreian, P. (1974). On the connectivity of social networks. *Journal of Mathematical Sociology, 3,* 245-258.

Friedman, S. R. (1995). Promising social network research results and suggestions. In R. H. Needle, S. L. Coyle, S. Genser, & R. T. Trotter, II (Eds.), *Social network analysis, HIV prevention and drug abuse* (NIDA Monograph 151, pp. 196-215). Bethesda, MD: National Institute on Drug Abuse.

Ford, L. R., & Fulkerson, D. R. (1956). Maximum flow through a network. *Canadian Journal of Mathematics, 8,* 399-404.

Galaskiewicz, J., & Wasserman, S. (1993). Social network analysis: Concepts, methodology, and directions for the 1990s. *Sociological Methods & Research, 22,* 3-22.

Glover, F. (1989). Tabu search—Part 1. *ORSA Journal on Computing, 1,* 190-206.

Glover, F. (1990). Tabu search—Part 2. *ORSA Journal on Computing, 2,* 4-32.

Gomory, R. E., & Hu, T. C. (1964). Synthesis of a communication network. *Journal of SIAM (Appl Math), 12,* 348.

Hubbell, C. H. (1965). An input-output approach to clique identification. *Sociometry, 28,* 377-399.

Johnson, J. C. (1994). Anthropological contributions to the study of social networks: A review. In S. Wasserman & J. Galaskiewicz (Eds.), *Advances in social network analysis.* Thousand Oaks, CA: Sage.

Katz, L. (1953). A new status index derived from sociometric data analysis. *Psychometrika, 18,* 34-43.

Kilworth, P., & Bernard, H. R. (1974). CATIJ: A new sociometric and its application to a prison living unit. *Human Organization, 33,* 335-350.

Knoke, D., & Kuklinski, J. H. (1982). *Network analysis.* Beverly Hills, CA: Sage.

Latkin, C. A. (1995). A personal network approach to AIDS prevention. In R. H. Needle, S. L. Coyle, S. Genser, & R. T. Trotter, II (Eds.), *Social network analysis, HIV prevention and drug abuse* (NIDA Monograph 151, pp. 181-195). Bethesda, MD: National Institute on Drug Abuse.

Mokken, R. (1979). Cliques, clubs and clans. *Quality and Quantity, 13,* 161-173.

Panning, W. (1982). Fitting blockmodels to data. *Social Networks, 4,* 81-101.

Pasternak, B. (1976). *Introduction to kinship and social organization.* Englewood Cliffs, NJ: Prentice Hall.

Scott, J. (1991). *Social network analysis: A handbook.* Newbury Park, CA: Sage.

Seidman, S., & Foster, B. (1978). A graph theoretic generalization of the clique concept. *Journal of Mathematical Sociology, 6,* 139-154.

Stephenson, K., & Zelen, M. (1991). Rethinking centrality. *Social Networks, 13,* 81-101.

Taylor, M. (1969). Influence structures. *Sociometry, 32,* 490-502.

Trotter, R. T., Bowen, A. M., Baldwin, J. A., & Price, L. J. (1996). The efficacy of network based HIV/AIDS risk reduction programs in mid-sized towns in the United States. *Journal of Drug Issues, 26,* 591-606.

Trotter, R. T. II, Bowen, A. M., & Potter, J. M. (1995). Network models for HIV outreach and prevention programs for drug users. In R. H. Needle, S. L. Coyle, S. Genser, & R. T. Trotter, II (Eds.), *Social network analysis, HIV prevention and drug abuse* (NIDA Monograph 151, pp. 144-180). Bethesda, MD: National Institute on Drug Abuse.

Trotter, R. T. II, Potter, J. M., Bowen, A. M., & Jiron, D. (Traducción Arturo Ortiz). (1994). Enfoques Etnograficos y analisis de las redes sociales, para la creacion de programs de prevencion del uso de drogas y de VIH, en usarios activos. In *Las adicciones: Hacia un. enfoque multidisciplinario* (pp. 45-54). Consejo Nacional contra las Adicciones, Secretária de salud, Mexico. Mexico, DF.

Trotter, R. T. II, Rothenberg, R. B., & Coyle, S. (1995). Drug abuse and HIV prevention research: Expanding paradigms and network contributions to risk reduction. *Connections, 18*(1), 29-46.

Wasserman, S., & Faust, K. (1993). *Social network analysis: Methods and applications.* New York: Cambridge University Press.

SUGGESTED RESOURCES

There are five resources that will expand your knowledge and skills in network analysis. The following three books provide an excellent introduction and an in-depth exploration of networks.

Knoke, D., & Kuklinski, J. H. (1982). *Network analysis.* Beverly Hills, CA: Sage.

This book provides an excellent rapid introduction to social network analysis. It defines social networks in clear and concise ways, and it provides definitions and explanations for the most basic types of social network data collection, concepts, and analysis strategies.

Johnson, J. C. (1994). Anthropological contributions to the study of social networks: A review. In S. Wasserman & J. Galaskiewicz (Eds.), *Advances in social network analysis* (pp. 113-151). Thousand Oaks, CA: Sage.

This chapter provides an excellent summary of all of the recent advances in network analysis in anthropology. It briefly discusses the history of ethnographic network analysis, provides an overview of the theories being explored, and discusses new directions for this type of research.

The other chapters in the book provide a very useful comparative overview of how social network analysis has developed in other social science disciplines.

Wasserman, S., & Faust, K. (1993). *Social network analysis: Methods and applications.* New York: Cambridge University Press.

This book provides you with a thorough introduction to network analysis, and an in-depth description of the theory, methods, and analytical strategies for all but the most obscure approaches to social network research. It is an excellent resource for everyone from beginners to very advanced scholars.

There are two computer programs available that are highly useful to network researchers. One, ANTHROPAC, has a small number of routines available for creating network questionnaires and doing some data manipulation. The other, UCINET IV, is designed specifically for conducting many of the basic types of social network data analysis.

Borgatti, S. P. (1996). *ANTHROPAC 4.0.* Natick, MA: Analytic Technologies.

ANTHROPAC provides ethnographers with a set of analytical tools for conducting rapid assessment studies and for collecting and analyzing several different types of cognitive data (e.g., pilesorts, triads tests, scaling, etc.). It allows ethnographers to develop questionnaires in the field, enter and modify data sets, and analyze a number of different types of data sets. There are several statistical routines available that are useful in analyzing personal network data as well as some social network data sets.

Borgatti, S. P., Everett, M. G., & Freeman, L. C. (1992). *UCINET IV Version 1.00.* Columbia, SC: Analytic Technologies.

This program allows researchers to enter social network data, transform those data into several different configurations that are useful for intensive analysis, and conduct most of the basic types of social network analysis that are routinely done in a social network research project. The manual for the program is an excellent reference source both for theory and for the algorithms that are used to analyze these data.

2 ━●━●━●━

MAPPING SPATIAL DATA

Ellen K. Cromley

THE SPATIAL PERSPECTIVE

Spatial data analysis and mapping are essential tools in the ethnographer's toolkit. The communities, villages, schools, and other social settings that the ethnographer studies do not function in a vacuum. They exist in particular environments that are both natural and human-made. The daily activity patterns of individuals are often constrained by the contemporary geography of the community, the culmination of earlier human-environment interactions. From the point of view of the individuals who live in a community, in the short term, the attributes of that community's environment are essentially fixed. In the long term, however, individuals and organizations can be agents of environmental or social change. From the viewpoints of the organizations serving a community, the geographical dimensions of their activities can be a major factor affecting how well the organizations function both in the present and in the future.

Most ethnographic research focuses on populations of individuals, although other units of analysis are possible (see Book 1 for a discussion of units of analysis; Bernard, 1994, pp. 35-36; LeCompte & Preissle, 1993). **Spatial data** are additional to other data values describing other attributes of the objects we are studying (Bailey & Gatrell, 1995,

The Spatial Perspective
•
Spatial Dimensions of Community
•
Spatial Dimensions of Individual Life
•
Collecting Data on Activity Spaces
•
Implications of Activity Data Collection
•
Spatial Dimensions of Community Institutions
•
Spatial Sampling
•
Mapping Spatial Data
•
The Power of Maps

Definition:
Spatial data are data on the relative locations of units of analysis

51

p. xi). For most anthropologists, the relevant space is a geographic space, a region on the earth's surface. Spatial analysis of geographic data is concerned with the relationships among individuals or other objects located on the earth's surface—in particular, those relationships that vary when the locations of the objects change (Gatrell, 1983, p. 2). "Spatial data analysis is involved when data are spatially located *and* explicit consideration is given to the possible importance of their spatial arrangement in the analysis or interpretation of results" (Bailey & Gatrell, 1995, p. 8).

Graphic and cartographic (mapped) representation and analysis of data make it possible to go beyond statistical representation. It is possible to define a number of different data sets that are statistically the same (same number of observations, same arithmetic mean, and so on) but graphically different (see Figure 2.1). Similarly, we can observe two pairs of variables with identical scatterplots, correlation coefficients, and class breaks for mapping, but distinctly different spatial patterns (see Figure 2.2). These displays show the distinction between statistical measures, such as frequency, and geographical patterns, such as locational arrangement, and they highlight the additional knowledge that can be gained by understanding spatial relationships among the units of analysis. Most statistical methods assume that the observational units "represent independent pieces of evidence about the relationship under study" (Bailey & Gatrell, 1995, p. 4). Spatial analysis enables us to consider the possible importance of neighborhood or environmental or other spatial-contextual influences.

The purpose of this chapter is to define and illustrate the usefulness of spatial concepts and methods for research in culturally different or culturally complex settings. The underlying theme is that an explicit understanding of the spatial aspects of human-environment relationships in a community can enhance ethnographic research. Maps are

I		II		III		IV	
X	Y	X	Y	X	Y	X	Y
10.00	8.04	10.00	9.14	10.00	7.46	8.00	6.58
8.00	6.95	8.00	8.14	8.00	6.77	8.00	5.76
13.00	7.58	13.00	8.74	13.00	12.74	8.00	7.71
9.00	8.81	9.00	8.77	9.00	7.11	8.00	8.84
11.00	8.33	11.00	9.26	11.00	7.81	8.00	8.47
14.00	9.96	14.00	8.10	14.00	8.84	8.00	7.04
6.00	7.24	6.00	6.13	6.00	6.08	8.00	5.25
4.00	4.26	4.00	3.10	4.00	5.39	19.00	12.50
12.00	10.84	12.00	9.13	12.00	8.15	8.00	5.56
7.00	4.82	7.00	7.26	7.00	6.42	8.00	7.91
5.00	5.68	5.00	4.74	5.00	5.73	8.00	6.89

For all four datasets:

$N = 11$
Mean of X's = 9.0
Mean of Y's = 7.5
Equation of regression line: $Y = 3 + 0.5X$
Standard error of estimate of slope = 0.118
$t = 4.24$
Sum of squares $X - \overline{X} = 110.0$
Regression sum of squares = 27.50
Residual sum of squares of Y = 13.75
Correlation coefficient = 0.82
$R^2 = 0.67$

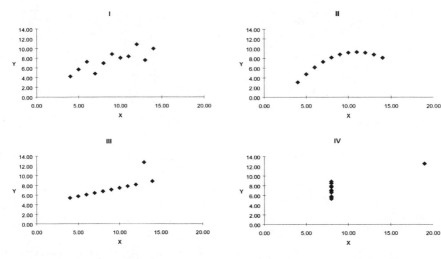

an important, although not the only, means for making spatial relationships explicit.

The first part of the chapter introduces key geographic concepts referring to the spatial dimensions of communities, individuals, and organizations, and it illustrates the use of these concepts in ethnographic research. Particular em-

Figure 2.1. The differences in four datasets shown in the table and having the same statistical properties are revealed by graphs. SOURCE: Adapted from Anscombe (1973).

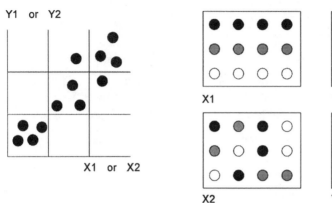

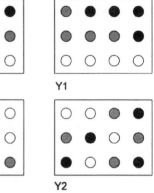

Figure 2.2. Two pairs of variables (X1,Y1 and X2,Y2) for 12 cases have identical scatterplots but very different spatial arrangements of the cases even when mapped using the same class breaks.
SOURCE: Adapted from Monmonier (1996).

phasis is placed on identification of the study area, spatial sampling, and identification of community needs through analysis of spatially referenced data. The second part of the chapter describes types of maps, critical components of maps, and techniques for mapping spatially referenced data, including geographic information systems (GIS). Ethical considerations in the collection, representation, and use of spatial data are discussed in the final part of the chapter.

SPATIAL DIMENSIONS OF COMMUNITY

Study Areas as Regions

Definition: A community is a group of people that interacts in characteristic ways based on shared values to meet common needs

The ethnographic case study focuses on the **community**, village, school, or other social unit (Johnston, Gregory, & Smith, 1994, pp. 80-81). Because daily human interaction has, until very recently, required people to be in the same place at the same time, there has usually been a strong spatial dimension to the understanding of community. Most definitions of community include the sharing of a localized territorial space as a key element. Communities are thus recognized as both social and spatial-temporal systems. **Community space** is the territory defined by the set of locations where the interactions of interest take place, including the homes of participants.

The interactions that typically occur within a community are not equally likely to occur everywhere within the community space. The time-space of the community has nested within it personal and group spaces that are defined, in part, by the rules of behavior associated with them. Most communities recognize the personal spaces of individuals, the range of conversation and social interaction space, and the range of public space beyond (Hall, 1966; Jakle, Brunn, & Roseman, 1976). In addition, we can identify socially sanctioned private places providing regular inhabitants with freedom from observation or demands by others, as well as socially sanctioned public places with freedom of access but a set of behavioral expectations. Private places generally include some part of an individual's home but may include other places, such as a social club, in which the regular inhabitants enjoy a degree of privacy and control. Control over public territory creates jurisdictions or administrative regions.

Introducing the spatial perspective into ethnographic research begins by describing the configuration of the community space and documenting where the interactions of interest occur. An early step in ethnographic research design, after formulation of the theoretical problem, is selection of an appropriate method and study site (Bernard, 1994, p. 102; see also the discussion in Books 1, 2, and 3 of strategies for making these decisions). The identification of the study area involves the ethnographer in defining a region. A **region** is an area of earth-space with attributes that differentiate it from surrounding areas (Johnston et al., 1994, pp. 506-509). In defining a study area, we are differentiating the places where observations will be made from the places where they will not. How the study area boundaries are drawn will affect what the researcher observes.

Definition: Community space is defined as the locations in which social interactions take place

Definition: A region has attributes that differentiate it from surrounding areas

Cross Reference: Book 1 also discusses ways to create boundaries around the population to be studied

To understand the issues involved in defining the study area, it is necessary to understand the different ways in which regions are constructed. The region is one of the most important constructs in geography, and there are a number of different ways to define regions. One type of region, the **formal region,** is defined by the presence or absence of one or more attributes (see Figure 2.3). In this definition, the regional boundaries are determined based on the researcher's understanding of the underlying spatial distribution of the units of observation with the attributes of interest, and the identified areas are considered homogeneous with respect to the attributes. A soil region is an example of a formal region based on analysis of samples taken at various locations and analyzed for soil type. A residential area of houses built at the same time might also be considered a formal region.

 Definition:
A formal region is defined by its attributes

Another type of region is the **functional region.** A functional region is defined by flows or interactions (see Figure 2.3). In this definition, the region is organized around nodes that are linked to the periphery by flows of people, goods, or information. An example of a functional region is a store's market area or a hospital discharge area. The boundaries of functional regions are often fuzzy.

 Definition:
A functional region is defined by flows of people, goods, or information

A third type of region, the **administrative region,** is a type of formal region in the sense that it is identified based on nominal data (see Figure 2.3). An area on the surface of the earth is either in or out of an administrative region. In Figure 2.3, the region's boundary distinguishes "in the Town of West Hartford" from "not in the Town of West Hartford." The boundaries of administrative regions are well defined, usually legally defined and even demarcated. Nevertheless, there is a very important difference from other regional boundaries in what the boundaries of administrative regions represent.

Definition:
The administrative region is defined by legal boundaries, without regard for the distribution of objects or flows within them

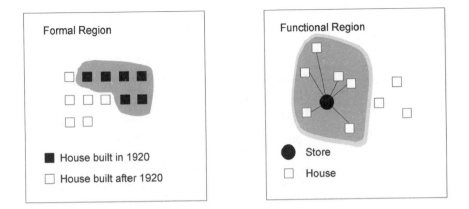

The boundary of the administrative region is rarely drawn based on an understanding of the underlying geographical distribution of objects or flows. Indeed, it would be difficult to develop a boundary that would respect all of the widely varying distributions of different objects and flows on the earth's surface. Administrative boundaries are, instead, generally arbitrary. As a consequence, administrative regions are usually not internally homogeneous with respect to an attribute even though they may look like formal regions when mapped. Population, for example,

Figure 2.3.
Different types of regions.

Figure 2.4.
Uneven
geographical
distribution of
housing units
within
administrative
regions.

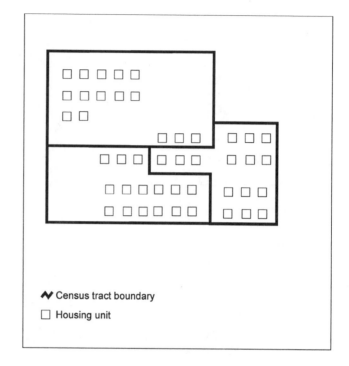

would not be uniformly distributed within a census tract
(see Figure 2.4). In addition, administrative regions often
arbitrarily partition the spatial distribution of the object
and flow phenomena we wish to study (see Figure 2.5).

Regions are important for describing, analyzing, and
administering geographic space. Understanding the nature
of regions is key to successful study area delimitation. The
goals of defining the study area are the following:

- To maximize internal homogeneity within the study area to
  ensure that as many of the units of analysis as possible are
  included

- To minimize flows across the study area boundary so that as
  many of the interactions of interest as possible are included
  (Foot, 1981, p. 14)

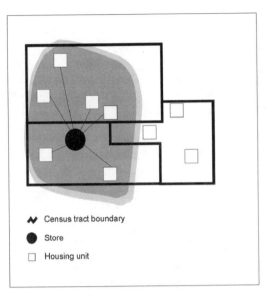

Figure 2.5.
Arbitrary partitioning of a functional region by administrative boundaries.

Ideally, the ethnographer would define a study area based on the distribution of the units of analysis and/or the patterns of interactions of interest. Unfortunately, most data collection and reporting units are based on administrative regions where boundaries may not reflect the distributions and flows of interest.

Defining the Study Area

Suppose that we are interested in an ethnographic study of the organization of public education in the United States. We want to study a town in Hartford County, Connecticut, because the population there is ethnically and socio-economically diverse. In the United States, public education is a function of state and local governments.

EXAMPLE 2.1   ━●━●━●━

HOW DIFFERENT CONCEPTS OF A REGION CAN BE USED TO
DEFINE THE STUDY AREA FOR ETHNOGRAPHIC RESEARCH

For our study, we select the Town of West Hartford (the town is the local unit of
government in most New England states) because of a debate occurring there on the
organization of the school system and how it serves different groups within the
community (Trotta, 1994). Among the issues were crowding and segregation within
the schools and how these problems might be addressed through redistricting. In this
case, the administrative region of the Town represents a formal region because the
services delivered by the Town's school system are provided within the Town boundaries. All schools—the locations of relevance where public education is provided—that
are part of the school system are located within the Town (see Figure 2.6).

Perhaps, however, the schools are not the units of analysis of interest for this study.
Because the issues of interest involve which grades, students, and teachers will be
assigned to which schools, it is important to look at the educational system as a
functional region in which the schools serve as nodes of activity for students and
teachers who travel from their home locations. In this case, we would want to talk to
individual teachers, students, parents, and administrators.

When we view the system in this way, we need to have an understanding of the
residential locations of teachers, administrators, and students, and how a school
reassignment would affect their daily travel and activity patterns. This requires us to
check the validity of our assumption that the Town boundaries describe the relevant
study area. Clearly, in a culture with high levels of personal mobility, it is unlikely that
all of the teachers and administrators would live within the Town. We might assume
that all of the students in the system would live in West Hartford, given the nature of
the administrative boundary. Anecdotal evidence, however, suggests that there is
significant but unquantified movement of students from neighboring towns into
adjacent school systems, including West Hartford (Rocha, 1994).

━●━●━●━

In this sense, the functional space of the West Hartford
school system extends beyond the borders of the Town. The

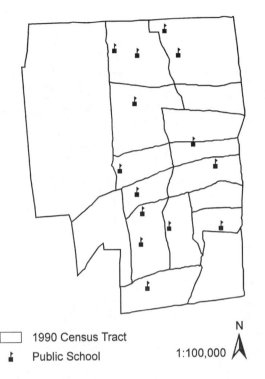

Figure 2.6. Public school locations in the town of West Hartford.

☐ 1990 Census Tract

⚑ Public School

1:100,000

N
⋀

magnitude of these flows of teachers and students and the participants' perceptions of the school district space are something that the ethnographer will have to take into account in defining the study area and the units of observation that will be included. The spatial perspective on the interactions that define communities is grounded in an understanding of the daily travel and activity patterns of the community members and how these influence their views of space.

Ethnographers can use maps in many other ways. Table 2.1 displays the role that maps can play in a number of issues that interest ethnographers, and it also lists questions that ethnographers must consider when using maps in their research.

(text continues on page 66)

TABLE 2.1 Using Maps in Community-Based Research Projects

Research Task	Questions to Consider	Role of Map	Data Collection and Mapping
Define the study area	What is the community I am studying? Is the study area best defined as a formal, functional, or administrative region for the purposes of my study? Do I need to show multiple views of the study area? Do the members of this community occupy a single contiguous region, or are they dispersed? What scale map is needed to represent the entire study area? What scale map is needed to represent the level of detail required by the study? Do I need more than one map or maps at different scales? Which symbols should I use to represent the features of interest?	Provides a basis for study area delimitation and for reference by showing the distribution of a feature of interest on the earth's surface, flows of interest on the earth's surface, or administrative regions of interest on the earth's surface	Acquire base map or maps at the appropriate scales by purchasing existing paper maps or digital spatial databases (see the Suggested Resources section) or by making your own Be aware of the accuracy and timeliness of the data represented on the paper map or in the digital spatial database Be aware of any restrictions on reproducing or copying and distributing paper maps and digital spatial databases

Research Task	Questions to Consider	Role of Map	Data Collection and Mapping
Describe the geographical distribution of community members	What is the geographical distribution of community members based on home location? Do I need to show the locations of individuals or individual housing units, or are aggregate counts and ratios for geographical areas sufficient? If I map residential locations of individuals, will I be violating confidentiality or putting community members at risk? How could the map be designed to prevent this?	Shows residential distribution of population and/or housing units by administrative region or researcher-defined formal or functional region Provides a framework for spatially stratified random sampling of community members	Population data tabulated for administrative regions and/or interpolated for researcher-defined regions Housing unit data tabulated for administrative regions and/or interpolated for researcher-defined regions Counts of housing units by region tabulated for administrative regions and/or interpolated for researcher-defined regions Investigate sources such as city directories Address-ranged street network database for geocoding addresses Acquire existing maps/images showing residential locations, including the following: • Cadastral maps showing property boundaries and building footprints • Air photos or satellite images showing locations of individual housing units • Insurance maps Are these data public data? Can they be redistributed?

(continued)

TABLE 2.1 Continued

Research Task	Questions to Consider	Role of Map	Data Collection and Mapping
Describe the activity spaces of community members by showing the locations of activity sites other than the home	What are the relevant activities (based on the underlying research questions) outside the home, and where do they take place? Are the timing, duration, and sequence of activities occurring at various locations important? Is the route from the home to the activity site and from activity site to activity site important? Do I need to explicitly include travel time and travel mode in data on activity patterns? If I map travel and activity patterns of individuals, will I be violating confidentiality or putting community members at risk? How could the map be designed to prevent this?	Geocode activity sites Plot geographical distributions of activity sites Show travel flows among activity sites Identify individuals who have similar travel and activity patterns by map comparison	Observation, diaries, or surveys of individuals to collect travel and activity data Investigate sources such as city directories and gazetteers for locations of activity sites Address-ranged street network database for geocoding addresses Acquire existing maps/images showing activity locations, including the following: • Cadastral maps showing property boundaries and building footprints • Air photos or satellite images showing locations of individual structures • Insurance maps Maps showing activity sites like schools

Research Task	Questions to Consider	Role of Map	Data Collection and Mapping
Describe the locations of community organizations of interest	What are the relevant (based on the research questions) community organizations? Where are the facilities of these organizations located? How would I characterize the size, centrality, and level of integration of various facilities? Are there linkages between facilities? How can these be represented?	Show the geographical organization of community institutions, including locations and flows	Key informant interviews with organization representatives Archival research
Identify locational problems	Does the geographical organization of facilities cover the population? If new facilities are needed, where should they be located? Do people's social obligations make it difficult for them to coordinate their activities in time and space? If facility locations and schedules are changed, who will be positively and negatively affected?	Show the geographical relationships (proximity, accessibility) among community institutions and the people they serve Show geographical constraints on meeting service objectives (e.g., four schools cannot be located in such a way that no child is more than 2 miles from a school) Suggest solutions to geographical problems (e.g., locate a new facility, improve transportation, change the scheduling of activities, improve neighborhood quality) Be aware of the values expressed in maps	Measure the spatial relationships described in the data collected and represented on maps Use maps in the description of community problems

SPATIAL DIMENSIONS OF INDIVIDUAL LIFE

Understanding the Activity Space

 Key point   *When the unit of analysis in an ethnographic study is the individual person, introducing the spatial perspective into ethnographic research involves understanding the daily travel and activity patterns of the individuals and how their direct experience of the environment influences their perceptions of geographic space.* Studies of how people allocate their time to activities during the day have their origins in 19th-century studies of social conditions in cities (Anderson, 1971). Research that relies on **time budgets,** or systematic records of an individual's use of time over a given period, has been conducted in a wide range of fields for a wide variety of purposes, from market research to urban planning and design to investigation of cultural change (Golledge & Stimson, 1987). Although they use common data collection techniques, time studies "do not constitute a unified research field" (Anderson, 1971, p. 353).

Definition:
Time budgets are systematic records of an individual's use of time over a specific period

When the locations in which activities take place are incorporated into time budgets, they become **space-time budgets.** Although we can choose to view the spatial-temporal pattern of activities as a matter of individual choice, it is also possible to emphasize the spatial and temporal constraints implicit in the patterns that the budgets encode. In the short run, the individual faces a fixed-feature space. The attributes of the natural and built environment are given, and the individual must adapt his or her activity patterns to them. This issue, "the fate of the individual human being in an increasingly complicated environment," and the outlines of a model for exploring the time-space of the individual were considered by the geographer Torsten Hagerstrand (1970, p. 7).

Definition:
Space-time budgets are systematic records of an individual's use of time in a specific location over a period of time

Hagerstrand identifies three constraints on human movement in the environment and interaction:

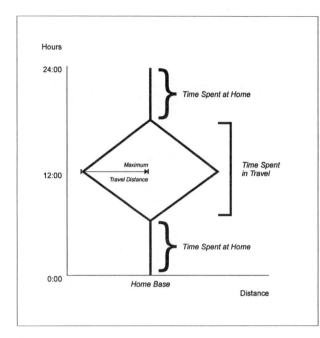

Figure 2.7. The daily time-space prism.
SOURCE: Adapted from Hagerstrand (1970).

- Capability constraints
- Coupling constraints
- Authority constraints

Definition: Capability constraint is anything that limits the geographic range of an individual

The need for people to have a permanent or semipermanent home base where they return periodically to rest and eat constrains the part of the environment where the individual is capable of being during any given day. The **daily time-space prism** is the island of the individual, the maximum area around the home base where the individual can travel before having to return home (see Figure 2.7). The size and shape of the time-space prism are affected by the mode of transportation available, the amount of time the person is required to spend at home, and the amount of time the person is required to spend at activity sites away from the home. The daily time-space prism will thus vary from culture to culture and from person to person, including those people who share the same home base.

Definition: Daily time-space prism is the maximum area around home base where the individual can travel before having to return home

Figure 2.8.
Coupling constraints.
SOURCE: Adapted
from Hagerstrand
(1970).

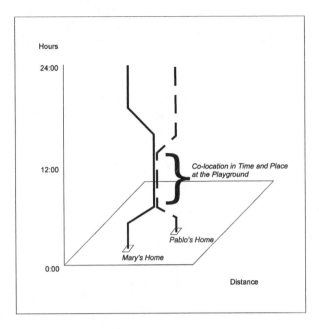

Definition:
Coupling
constraints define
limits on where,
when, and for how
long a person has to
join with others

Definition:
Authority
constraints are
imposed by those
with control over the
use of space who
limit timing and the
kinds of interaction
within a particular
space

The amount of time spent at particular locations is ruled by **coupling constraints**, which define where, when, and for how long a person has to join with others (see Figure 2.8). The time budget itself reflects the importance of clock and calendar as key mechanisms for organizing time in industrial and postindustrial societies. Activities requiring face-to-face interaction require colocation in time and space. Communication innovations such as the telephone require only co-"location" in time. The need for colocation has been viewed negatively, as a set of problems to be overcome, and positively, as a mechanism for enabling social activity and construction of social meaning (Dyck, 1990).

The final constraints affecting the environment of the person are **authority constraints**. Personal and public spaces represent a set of spatial domains where the priorities of particular individuals or groups for use of the space are enforced. Authority constraints are based upon which individuals or groups can legitimately expect their priorities to

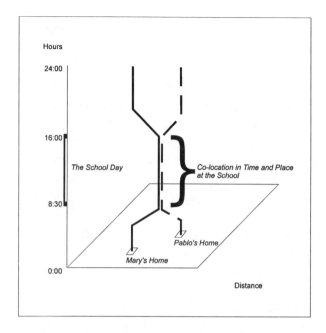

Figure 2.9.
Authority constraints.
SOURCE: Adapted
from Hagerstrand
(1970).

be enforced. Authority constraints limit and define the timing and nature of interactions that can occur within spatial domains (see Figure 2.9).

The constraints considered by Hagerstrand mean that access to resources or avoidance of hazards in the environment involve more than simple juxtapositions of features and populations. They involve "a time-space location which really allows the life-path to make the required detours" (Hagerstrand, 1970, p. 19). As Hagerstrand points out, for example, predetermined time tables exist for the school, and the schoolchild does not have the freedom to choreograph the activities of the day (p. 15). He emphasizes that travel and activity patterns may be particularly complicated for dependent members of households, such as children.

The **activity space** of the individual, the area in which time is spent, is built up out of daily travel and activity patterns and includes the home base, other activity sites, and the pathways connecting these locations (Johnston

Definition:
Activity
space is the
area in which
an individual
spends time

et al., 1994, p. 4). As such, elements in a person's activity space may be separated by areas that the person hardly knows at all because no time has been spent there. Direct personal contact with a place is an important means of acquiring spatial knowledge and a sense of place.

The environment of the person has an objective reality in the geographical locations where the person is observed or reported to be. The environment of the person also has a subjective reality in perception and assessment of the lived space. The spatial perspective on community, based on an understanding of the travel and activity patterns of its members, is enriched by consideration of individuals' geographic perspectives and experiences.

 Definition: Cognitive maps are bodies of information that people store about the location of things in physical space

Cognitive maps, as used in geography, are "long term stored information about the relative location of objects and phenomena in the everyday physical environment" (Garling, Book, & Lindberg, 1979, p. 200). The environments that are the basis for the individual's cognitive map may be known to exist or may be imagined, and they often represent a mix of information drawn from different periods of time (Golledge & Stimson, 1987, p. 72). Both cognitive and developmental approaches have been applied to the study of spatial cognition.

Spatial learning involves intellectual development (Piaget & Inhelder, 1967) as well as the acquisition of information over time, largely as a result of direct contact with the environment (Jakle et al., 1976, p. 93). In a developmental sense, spatial perception begins with awareness of perceived objects, location of the object in time and space, recognition of attributes of the object, and attachment of meaning to it (Golledge & Stimson, 1987, p. 53).

Some of the earliest research on cognitive mapping addressed the "imageability" of the environment. Lynch's (1960) work on the image of the city identified key elements of urban environments: paths, edges, districts, nodes, and landmarks. This work has been extended to the imaging of small local cultural areas or neighborhoods.

The **neighborhood** has a physical area readily identifiable on a map. Many cues used to identify neighborhoods are physical—housing types, land use, and density. The street network or other paths is the single most important factor used to identify neighborhood boundaries (Golledge & Stimson, 1987, p. 65). Although neighborhoods are physically demonstrable, it is not easy to define a neighborhood—in advance of studying it—based on specific area or population size criteria alone. The size and shape of the physical neighborhood vary from place to place and culture to culture depending on the location and size of the settlement in which the neighborhood is found, travel modes, household density, and patterns of interaction.

The neighborhood also has a social component. Local social interaction, social class, ethnic and racial origins, life cycle characteristics of the population, length of residence, and place of work have all been considered as factors defining neighborhoods. Level of education and social class affect the range of cues used to identify neighborhoods (Golledge & Stimson, 1987, p. 67) and their perceived size and complexity (Orleans & Schmidt, 1972).

The "imageability" of the environment is, according to Gulick (1966), more than just the recognition of physical features. It is a function of the individual's perception of the form of physical features in the landscape and the social or behavioral significance that the person attributes to the features. **Sense of place** refers to how people evaluate places and decide that they are distinctive based on their unique characteristics (Johnston et al., 1994, pp. 548-549). "Kilimanjaro" and "Paris" evoke a strong sense of meaning for many people, even those who have not directly experienced these places. Sense of place also develops as a deep attachment through experience and memory to the places where

Definition: Neighborhood is defined as a physical area with shared social features

Definition: Sense of place means the assessment of a place as distinctive based on unique characteristics

we live (Eyles, 1985). In both cases, objective aspects of location are combined with subjective experience, direct or indirect. Most recently, attention has been focused on how sense of place is created by intention in contemporary architecture and planning (Ley, 1989). This may be accomplished by preserving the physical features of derelict structures in the rehabilitation process but assigning a new use to the space.

Cognitive maps and geographical experiences have been explored in many populations, from children (Aitken, 1994) through the elderly (Rowles, 1986). As a process that develops throughout the lifespan in all humankind (Siegel, 1981), cognitive mapping is potentially relevant in a wide range of ethnographic research. A full treatment of research methods for investigating how people learn about the environment, perceive it, and make locational decisions is not possible in this chapter (for more information, see Golledge & Stimson, 1987, 1997).

COLLECTING DATA ON ACTIVITY SPACES

Ways to Record Data on Activity Spaces

■ Observations
■ Diaries
■ Recalled data elicited via interviews
■ Games

Several techniques have been used for gathering information on people's travel and activity patterns during a specified period of time (Golledge & Stimson, 1987, p. 155). The main data collection methods for activity analysis are the observational method (observations in the field conducted by the field researcher), the diary method (kept either by the field researcher or by the participant), or the recall method (in which researchers interview participants).

Researchers have also employed game-based methods, often postdiary or postinterview, to explore the impact of changes in the contingencies of decision-making environment (Jones, 1979). A researcher might, for example, ask how a person would allocate additional free time.

> ### Strategies for Collecting Activity Records
>
> ■ Continuous direct observation
> ■ Continuous direct observation of sampled activity units
> ■ Direct observation of a sample of subjects and times
> ■ Subject recall
> ■ Subject record keeping
> ■ Personal recall interviews on activities and time spent

Data collected by these methods can be used to construct activity records of four main types (Anderson, 1971, p. 356):

1. Time budgets (describing allocation of time to activities)
2. Space-time budgets (describing allocation of time to activities engaged in at specific locations)
3. Contact records (describing face-to-face and person-to-person communication)
4. Travel records (describing the temporal sequence of trips from origins to destinations, including the purposes of the trips and the modes of transportation but ignoring allocation of time to activities at the destinations)

Activity records present some challenging problems for data collection and analysis (Ricci et al., 1995). The most important are the validity and reliability of time-space data and the cost of collecting them. Continuous direct observation (i.e., the field researcher observes and records in a diary how and when people spend their time) can yield accurate and representative information. In these "broad-focus" time-use studies (Grossman, 1984), all activities are observed over a sufficient time period to capture daily and other periodic variations in activity patterns.

EXAMPLE 2.2   ━●━●━

CONTINUOUS DIRECT OBSERVATION OF ACTIVITIES

A study of dietary intake and energy expenditure by Edmundson attempted to observe and record how and where people spent their time. Over a 1-year period, four researchers continuously observed and recorded activities of 54 Javanese villagers almost to the minute for 14 hours per day. This represented 324 researcher-days of continuous observation (Edmundson, 1976).

━●━●━

This method of data collection, however, poses ethical and practical problems. The ethical issue of surveillance of individuals is discussed in the final section of this chapter. The practical problems are basically problems of cost in collecting and managing the voluminous databases that result. In the case of the West Hartford school system, elementary school enrollment during the 1994-1995 school year was reported as 4,100 (Department of Education, 1994). It would be extremely expensive to observe directly all of these students throughout the school year. It probably also would not be necessary. Valid data on school population activity patterns can be obtained by studying a sample. Spatial sampling techniques for selecting individuals to be included in travel and activity data collection efforts are reviewed in a later section of this chapter dealing with spatial sampling.

Two alternatives to broad-focus direct continuous observation are broad-focus time-space studies by direct observation of a sample of subjects and times (Johnson, 1975) or direct continuous observation of only selected activities for a limited period during the day (Ruddle, 1974; Smith, 1981). The first alternative limits the number of observations, as illustrated by the following example.

DIRECT OBSERVATION OF ACTIVITIES FOR A SAMPLE OF DAYS AND TIMES

In Johnson's study of time allocation in a Machiguenga community in Peru, 13 households were selected as a sample. The sample was divided into two groups, each group observed on an alternating basis. A random numbers table was used to select days and hours for group observation in advance. During the designated observation period, the effort was made to locate and observe all individuals within the group and to record each individual's activity at the time of observation. The hours of observation were confined to daylight. Over a 10-month period, observations were made on 134 different days, yielding 3,495 records for individuals in the sample households. Percentage-of-time estimates were developed by dividing the number of observations of a particular activity by the total number of observations of all activities (Johnson, 1975).

━●━●━

The number of observations that must be made to ensure a representative sample in this type of study can be quite large, depending, in part, on how frequently activities occur (Bernard & Killworth, 1993).

A second alternative limits the number of activities and observations. Studies that focus on specific activities can be valuable, but care must be taken in the use of this approach, particularly for comparative research. Differing viewpoints among field researchers as to which activities count as "work," "school," or "leisure" can have "negative implications for cross-cultural, cross-spatial and cross-temporal comparisons" (Carlstein, 1982, p. 332). In West Hartford, "public elementary education" means tax-supported kindergarten through fifth grade education available to all residents of the town. In other communities in the state, elementary schools may serve a different age range of students. In other countries, public elementary education might mean something still different. In Ghana, for example, children must be 6 years of age before they can attend public primary school and can attend until age 12.

In some cases, the field researcher will not be directly observing and recording activity data as the activity takes place. Instead, the subjects themselves keep records or recall and verbally report on their activities. Adopting the data collection technique of asking individuals to keep their own activity records enables researchers to collect much more data than they could by direct continuous observation. It also avoids the ethical issues of surveillance and the practical problems of individuals altering their daily travel and activity patterns because they are being observed by the field researcher. The disadvantages of the diary kept by the research subject arise when the research subjects are illiterate or otherwise incapable of recording events accurately, when the time-reckoning system used by study subjects does not match the system (hours and minutes, days, months) represented in the diary, and when records are required to be kept over a long period of time. People also are notoriously careless in recording daily events meticulously. The quality and completeness of the diaries has been observed to decline over time as respondents tire of recordkeeping—which has probably become a significant new activity in and of itself (Grossman, 1984). For these reasons, respondent diaries would probably be very difficult to implement among young elementary school children in West Hartford.

A final data collection technique for individual daily activity patterns is personal or face-to-face interviewing with a questionnaire that asks respondents to recall activities and the amounts of time spent on them for one or more days prior to the time of the interview. This technique has numerous drawbacks.

- Respondents who do not have or do not usually rely on time-keeping devices have difficulty stating precisely how much time was spent on various activities.

- If the recall period is extended weeks or months, it is difficult to incorporate periodic changes or cycles in activities.

- Respondents may overestimate the amount of time spent on arduous activities while understating the amount of time spent on leisure or discretionary activities (Grossman, 1984).

One review of recall studies concluded that half of what respondents report is inaccurate in some way (Bernard, Killworth, Kronfeld, & Sailor, 1984).

To enhance the validity and reliability of the activity data, the researcher must understand the local context and have clearly defined research goals. The various data collection strategies can be and have been used individually and in combination to improve data quality.

Focal Sampling as an Alternative to Spot Sampling

Spot sampling is "the basis for time allocation studies in anthropology" (Bernard & Killworth, 1993, p. 207). Spot sampling is most easy to implement when the number of individuals in the sample for observation during any particular time period is kept small and when the activity sites where individuals will be observed are relatively close together in space so that individuals can be located easily. *If researchers must spend time in travel to observe activities directly for a large number of individuals in a large area, it may be impossible to make the required direct observations.* "To locate and observe the activities of numerous villagers from several different households within the same hour, with people scattered over the entire 39km² territory, would require a herculean effort" (Grossman, 1984, p. 452). In highly mobile, automobile-based societies, these problems would be magnified. Although recall can be used to fill in gaps, this may bias the data, particularly affecting inclusion of activities that occur at remote locations and of the travel

Definition:
Spot sampling
selects random
times during a
study period and
records behaviors
of individuals
during those times

Key point

effort that the individuals being studied must put into reaching those locations.

Spot sampling may understate time devoted to travel as an activity. Time spent in travel is a key component of the Hagerstrand model because time spent in travel is time that cannot be allocated to other in-home or out-of-home activities. Studies of time use often neglect time spent in travel altogether or simply incorporate it into the time effort put into other activities (Carlstein, 1982). This is a glaring problem, particularly in cross-cultural work or longitudinal research, because personal mobility varies greatly from culture to culture and over time.

EXAMPLE 2.4 ━●━●━

ACCOUNTING FOR TIME SPENT IN TRAVEL AS AN ACTIVITY

A study of changing time allocation patterns from 1968 to 1988 among adults 18 to 65 years old in metropolitan Washington, D.C. found that time spent at home decreased 80 minutes per day during the 20-year period. Thirty minutes of that time was accounted for by increased time at work, 20 minutes by increased time at other places, and 30 minutes by increased time spent in travel (Levinson & Kumar, 1995).

Although spot sampling may be valuable when the researcher is interested only in gross allocation of time to different activities and not *where* activities regularly occur, spot sampling creates problems when the researcher is interested in temporal and spatial patterns because spot sampling does not place the observed activity in its temporal and spatial context. In the case of redistricting West Hartford elementary schools, this context is important. Any redistricting that significantly alters travel time to school for children in either direction (increasing it or decreasing it) would obviously affect the amount of time that children could devote to *other* (nonschool) activities during the day and that parents need to devote to providing care for children when they are not in school (Jones, 1979). In this case, it would be important to obtain data on before- and after-school activities as well. These activities would be of varying duration and might be missed under different spot sampling scenarios.

As Hagerstrand's model suggests, spot samples basically support gross allocation of time analyses (what people spent time on). Because of the spatial biases that can be introduced when activities occur over large geographical areas, they are less useful than are focal samples for creating valid data for activity space (where people spend time) analyses. **Focal sampling** involves sampling individuals, not times, and then developing relatively complete travel and activity records for a period of time. Respondents who have similar travel and activity patterns in similar locations can then be grouped.

The temporal span of observation and data collection is of critical importance. In the case of the West Hartford school system, students never attend classes on Saturday or Sunday. On the other days of the week, the school day begins at 8:40 a.m. and ends at 3:20 p.m., except on Wednesdays, when students are dismissed at 1:50 p.m. so that teachers can engage in staff development activities. Other exceptions to the regular pattern include holidays, summer vacation, and days when the school schedule changes because of inclement weather. Observations on any single day will obviously not capture this rich temporal variation in the schedule for the school as a whole, let alone variations that might affect individual students and teachers.

When an activity being observed takes place in a particular spatial domain where activity is restricted to certain times, the broad temporal parameters of activity can be determined in advance for many individuals simply by examining the rules for use of space enforced by the individual or organization that controls the domain. In the case

Definition:
Focal sampling samples individuals and follows them over time

Key point

of the West Hartford school system, these data can be obtained by purposive sampling and interviewing of school officials. In the chapter section "Defining the Study Area," the geographical problem of defining the school district boundary as representative of where students actually come from (i.e., assuming that no students have home locations outside the school district) was discussed. Analogous to this is the temporal problem of the official school day period (the official time boundary) as representative of when students actually arrive at and depart from the school. The schedule rules of the system are perhaps more important for suggesting an appropriate temporal sampling scheme for data collection to capture temporal variation in activity schedules than for describing actual travel and activity patterns of individual students. For other specific activities that are not "regulated," important aspects of the general timing and periodicity of the activities may not be easy to determine in advance of data collection, and bias may result as a consequence.

IMPLICATIONS OF ACTIVITY DATA COLLECTION FOR ANALYSIS

Much of the analysis of individual activity data is concerned only with gross allocation of time to different classes of activity. This approach masks other important dimensions of human spatial behavior, including the sequencing and duration of activity episodes in time and space, and how these are affected by and affect the spatial arrangement of sites in the individual's activity space. For spatial analysis, these sequencing, duration, and arrangement patterns are key. Whenever activities occurring in sequence do not occur at the same location, some transportation time cost is incurred in switching from one activity to another (Hensher

& Stopher, 1979, p. 12). Two women may each work 8 hours per day, but if one has to be away from work and at home from noon to 1:00 p.m. to feed and care for children, she has a very different and less flexible activity pattern in time and space.

━●━●━

EXAMPLE 2.5

LACK OF TIME VERSUS INTERRUPTION AS BARRIERS TO ENGAGING IN AN ACTIVITY

One focal study of breastfeeding in a population of low-income urban mothers concluded that time constraints were not a "real" barrier to exclusive breastfeeding but might be "*perceived* [italics added] as time-consuming not so much because of the *total* amount of time required, but because it is more likely to interrupt the mother's activity (if the activity is perceived to be incompatible with breastfeeding), thereby causing her to 'lose' time" (Cohen, Haddix, Hurtado, & Dewey, 1995).

━●━●━

"Interruption" is just as real a time barrier to performing certain activities as total lack of time. In another research context, analysts observed that although average duration of time spent on travel increased over a 20-year study period, the temporal and spatial patterns of travel also became more complex, with an increase in multipurpose trips and a change in the time-of-day distribution of work and nonwork trips, especially those made by car (Levinson & Kumar, 1995).

When so much effort will be put into the collection of rich data on the nature, frequency, sequence, duration, and location of activities, reliance solely on analytical techniques such as aggregate time allocation seems an unjustifiable, though common, practice. By contrast, time-space path data are a kind of event-history data indicating the timing of moves in a sequence (Tuma & Hannan, 1984). If events may occur at any time, the process generating the event data is a continuous-time, discrete-state, stochastic process.

Definition:
Stochastic
process models
are statistical
models that
describe sequences
of outcomes in terms
of their probability of
happening

Stochastic process models are built using inferential statistics (Johnston et al., 1994, pp. 594-595). These models are based on the idea that the same process can produce a very large number of different outcomes. Stochastic models are different from deterministic models that can yield only one outcome for one set of inputs.

In an effort to explain why particular individuals engage in activities at particular locations, geographers have developed these kinds of models of spatial search and destination choice. One particular type, the Markov process model, has been used extensively to examine search and learning processes (Golledge & Brown, 1967) and alternative structures of travel behavior (Hensher & Stopher, 1979). These models require the researcher to define a set of possible *states* or conditions in which an individual might be at various points in time. For example, "married," "divorced," and "single" might define a set of states. In geographical analyses, "states" generally refers to locations. Based on a matrix of probabilities of changing from one state to another state, the probability of an individual being in a particular state at a particular time can be defined. Markov models have also been used to address sampling and analysis problems of time budget data (Rugg & Buech, 1990).

In studies of human travel and activity patterns, states represent the activity sites people visit during the course of their daily lives. Most households function as organizations from a single activity site—the home base—whose location is permanent or semipermanent. The home is one "state"

 Key point where a person could be. *Community organizations and institutions also function in space. Their operations are based at particular locations and imply flows of staff and clients.* As the next section reveals, the spatial organization of their activities is an important component of communities, reflecting and influencing patterns of social interaction.

SPATIAL DIMENSIONS OF COMMUNITY INSTITUTIONS

Dimensions of Service Provision

Community organizations function in time and space as much as individuals. Some organizations, such as schools, operate at one or more fixed locations. These service centers represent nodes in the activity spaces of service providers and service users. Other individuals or organizations that provide services to people move around (the visiting nurse or physician making a house call, the home-delivered meals service, the postal delivery service). These services' activity patterns can be evaluated using time budget approaches like those described for analyzing individual travel and activity patterns. In addition to the location or set of locations where services are provided, there are other dimensions of community institutions (Alter, 1988) that have geographical implications.

Definition: Community organizations are locations from which people obtain services and satisfy physical, social, or economic needs

The relationships between total **size of an organization** or system (measured as the number of service sites) and capacity or volume of service are important but not always straightforward. In the case of the West Hartford school system, there were 10 elementary schools in 1994-1995 (see Figure 2.10; Department of Education, 1994). Community organizations located in communities of similar size can provide varying volumes of service depending upon eligibility requirements and intake.

Definition: Size of an organization is defined as the number of service sites an organization has

When there are threshold requirements before a facility can be opened (e.g., no elementary school should serve fewer than 100 students) and/or minimum standards for service delivery (e.g., no child should live more than 5 miles from an elementary school), the number, location, and capacities of service centers will be strongly influenced by the underlying geographical distribution of the population to be served. In fact, depending on the distribution of children, it may not be feasible geographically to meet both

Figure 2.10. Public
school locations in
the town of West
Hartford showing the
hierarchy of educa-
tional services.

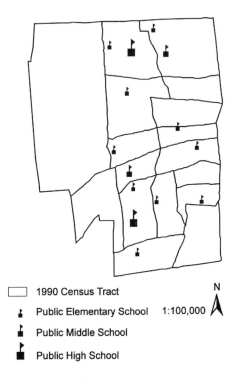

	1990 Census Tract
♟	Public Elementary School 1:100,000
♟	Public Middle School
▮	Public High School

N

the threshold and the minimum service standard just identified. This would happen if there were a small residential
neighborhood located more than 5 miles from an existing
elementary school with too few students to meet the threshold requirement. If state law required the provision of
public elementary school services to the children, one of the
requirements would have to be broken. Either taxpayers
would pay a subsidy to run the small school, or students
would pay in excessive travel time to school.

 Definition:
Centrality
refers to the
number of users
flowing through
one organization
relative to other
organizations

Centrality is another dimension of community organizations. When the total volume of users flows through a
single organization, that organization has a high degree of
centrality. There is a strong relationship between differen-
tiation of activity functions and degree of centrality. The

West Hartford public school system as a whole provides several different levels of educational services: elementary school education, middle school education, and secondary or high school education. The middle and high school services are more centralized than are the elementary services because a higher proportion of students flow through those schools. There are 10 elementary schools but only two middle schools and two high schools in the system (see Figure 2.10).

The geographical relationships among service centers with varying degrees of centrality are the focus of **central place theory** (Christaller, 1933/1966), as well as subsequent research on human settlement systems and public and private service systems (Foot, 1981; Ghosh & Rushton, 1987). When a population is uniformly distributed, those service centers with smaller threshold requirements will be more common in the landscape and spaced relatively close together, as the elementary schools in West Hartford are. Those activity sites with larger threshold requirements will be less common in the landscape and spaced relatively far apart. The service areas of small activity sites are sometimes nested in the service areas of larger activity sites.

Integration refers to the linkages or interdependencies among units within a system. A **forward linkage** is a linkage to a supplier of service. In the school system, the linkage from an elementary school to a middle school is a forward linkage. The linkage from a high school to a middle school would be a backward linkage. In the case of a public school system in the United States, alternative pathways through the service hierarchy do not generally exist. Students from a particular neighborhood are assigned to a particular elementary school and will move on to a particular middle school and a particular high school. For other systems of community organizations, alternative pathways may exist.

Definition:
Central place theory explains the size and space of service centers

Definition:
Integration is the interdependency among units in a system

Definition:
A forward linkage is a linkage to a supplier of service

Collecting Data on Community Organizations

The activity sites where people travel to obtain some good or service or to satisfy some physical, social, or economic need can be thought of, loosely, as community organizations. A major difficulty in studying how people relate to these organizations is that there are wide variations from culture to culture and from time to time in how these organizations are governed and function. A human service that might be provided under central government auspices in one place is provided by a local unit of government in another and may be left to the market in still another. In countries such as the United States, there have been important shifts in responsibility between the public and private sectors over time (Fuchs, 1996). Numerous typologies of human service and community organizations have been developed within the social work and public administration literature (Gans & Horton, 1975; Rabin & Steinhauer, 1988).

These distinctions are important because they affect the availability of data on community organizations that are critical to evaluating access or power to use. Penchansky and Thomas (1981) identify five dimensions of access: availability, accessibility, affordability, accommodation, and acceptability.

1. *Availability:* the relationship of volume and type of activity to volume and type of community need
2. *Accessibility:* the relationship between the location of supply and the location of users, taking into account the factors that affect human travel behavior
3. *Affordability:* the relationship between the cost of obtaining the service once the users are on site and the users' ability to pay
4. *Accommodation:* the relationship between the manner in which the supply resources are organized to accept users

(hours of operation, telephone communication, etc.) and the users' perceptions of and abilities to adapt to these patterns

5. *Acceptability:* the relationship between users' attitudes about characteristics of providers and providers' attitudes about users

Information to evaluate the accessibility of the locations of community organizations' offices or service centers usually is relatively easy to obtain from published directories or other archival sources, from government agencies if the service is publicly provided, or from direct observation and knowledge of the study area. The nature of the organization more seriously affects availability of data on the capacities of service providers, the nature of the service provided, utilization, and service users within the community. Organizations may not want to collect some forms of information or may not allow the information to be used.

When the provider is a government agency, there are often legally mandated reporting requirements, and these reports may constitute a useful data archive for the ethnographer. In the case of the West Hartford school system, for example, the Connecticut Department of Education publishes school district profiles and an education directory on an annual basis. These publications give locations of schools, enrollments, names and contact information for school officials, and financial or operating expense data such as the per-pupil expenditure and property tax base in the town.

Researchers working in the United States operate in a country with relatively strong requirements regarding freedom of information access and reporting. Federal government documents are not copyright protected in the United States. There is a federal depository institution program to disseminate data on government organizations to libraries around the United States, and these data are often available in multiple formats (print and digital). In other countries of the world, access to government data is much more likely to be restricted.

When the organizations are private, data availability may be even more restricted. Private organizations release some information in an effort to disseminate information about and market their services. However, organizations that compete for users will not wish to reveal their data on the fundamental aspects of their organizations (staffing, pricing, etc.). A consortium of private schools might publish a directory of private schools in Connecticut, but participation in these kinds of reporting is usually voluntary.

Even when an organization is willing to make data available about the organization, the locations of its service centers, and its operations, data on the individuals served by the organization may not be accessible. For example, the researcher may be interested in obtaining information on individual students in a school by interviewing them or obtaining information from their school records. This means that the research involves human subjects. Ethical constraints on access to information from human subjects served by various kinds of community organizations are enforced by institutional review boards (IRBs). The role of IRBs is discussed in detail in Books 1 and 6.

Cross Reference: The role of IRBs is discussed in greater detail in Books 1 and 6

Record-keeping by organizations has been influenced in many countries by the development of computer-based management information systems. Laws affecting disclosure of information by organizations will, as noted, vary from country to country. An important concept related to record-keeping law is confidentiality (Rabin & Steinhauer, 1988, pp. 396-401). Confidentiality laws are intended to protect relationships between service providers and service users, not to shield wrongdoing by organizations or individual providers.

In the United States, interestingly, common law did not provide a privilege against disclosure of private communications, because this privilege would inhibit the court's ability to reveal the whole truth through the adversarial process (Brakel, Parry, & Weiner, 1985). Even illness was at one time considered publicly known and disclosable. With attorney-client privilege as the precedent, however, legislative bodies began to authorize a confidentiality privilege for other types of relationships, including medical service providers and patients, balancing judicial access against privacy. In the United States, many social service providers do not enjoy privileged communication with their clients, and certain kinds of information (e.g., information on child abuse) are not privileged.

Disclosure laws also take into account affirmative record-keeping requirements. Without records, it is very difficult to document the delivery and review the quality of service provided. Thus, data will almost always be collected for individuals or individual contacts to meet affirmative record-keeping requirements, but it will almost always be reported in aggregates to avoid disclosure of confidential information. This has particular implications for geographic research.

Setting aside the institutional barriers to obtaining data on dimensions of community organization, services are notoriously hard to measure. It is often difficult to describe exactly the unit of service provided by a particular organization. For example, do we best measure educational service by the amount of time the teacher spends with each student or by the tasks in which the teachers and students engage? Do we evaluate services in terms of the money spent on service units or in terms of what clients actually achieve or gain from receiving the services?

Quality of service is even more difficult to measure. This is usually accomplished by measurement of outcomes. Here, too, it is not always clear what the most valid outcome is for assessing quality. In the case of the school system, is it the number of children who pass state mastery tests? Would it be the number of children who complete the educational program? These issues raise some important implications for the analysis of data collected on community organizations.

Although some archival data on community organizations' locations and operations may be available to the ethnographer, high-quality data on how organizations currently function will almost always need to be collected from or verified by directors and staff of the organizations. Key informant interviews and observations will be an important part of the data collection process (Bernard, 1995, pp. 165-179; see Book 2 for a discussion of such interviews). These ethnographic data collection techniques balance, supplement, and may replace the archival and other forms of data collection mentioned previously.

Cross Reference: Key informant interviewing and open-ended observations are discussed in Book 2

Analysis of Data Collected on Community Organizations

The spatial analysis of community organizations usually relies on modeling the organization as a network, including a set of nodes identifying the headquarters of the organization and the places where services are delivered, as well as a set of links representing the possible pathways connecting or linking the nodes in geographic space (see Figure 2.10). An important motivation for modeling the organization in this way is to explore potential opportunities for improving access to the organization and its operational efficiency.

In geography and regional science, this analysis has generally been accomplished by the application of normative modeling techniques. These techniques determine the maximum or minimum of a function. Unlike positive models relying on multivariate statistical methods to describe and analyze what is or was, normative models are concerned with what ought to be; they rely on mathematical programming methods. In particular, mathematical programming models are useful in attempts to maximize or minimize some function, such as total transportation cost of obtaining services given a set of constraints (Foot, 1981). For example, instead of describing the actual route that a school bus takes to collect and take students to school, normative models determine the optimal route. This would involve specifying an objective function, such as distance traveled, and finding the minimum value of the function subject to a set of constraints, such as the constraint that every student on the route must be picked up. If a researcher were evaluating the locational efficiency of a system of 10 schools, the p-median problem might be used to determine which candidate locations for schools should be selected to minimize the aggregate distance traveled from all households sending children to school. Although many early models specified single objectives, multiobjective mathematical program models have been developed (Malczewski & Orgyczak, 1995, 1996). Mathematical programming models are widely used in operations research. Geographers and regional scientists use these models in locational analysis, but most social scientists receive much less training in mathematical programming as a method of quantitative analysis than they do in multivariate statistical techniques.

There has been vigorous debate about the role of location theory in planning services, particularly in non-Western countries where the sociospatial circumstances are often very different (Rushton, 1984, 1988). Location-allocation models developed for the United States, for example, where there are high levels of personal mobility and a dense street network, might not be appropriate for a country like Ghana, where travel is difficult, especially in rural areas, and private transportation is rare (Oppong, 1996). The occurrence of a rainy season, which makes some road segments impassable during certain times of the year, means that any modeling effort based on the functioning of the transportation system during the dry season might produce disastrous results. Despite the limitations of single-objective mathematical programming models, normative modeling can provide some quantitative benchmarks for evaluating service delivery systems and exploring temporal and spatial constraints in service delivery.

Increasingly, the "solution space" for location problems such as siting, districting, and routing are being explored through *spatial decision support systems (SDSS)*. These computer-based systems provide decision makers with a tool for solving poorly or semistructured problems. Often, members of a community will express a variety of desires for service availability, including minimizing the cost of providing services while guaranteeing that everyone have a reasonable travel time to the service site. Through SDSS, it is possible to explore the trade-offs among various desires.

In a study of educational service districts in Iowa, for example, the planning group learned through modeling the problem with an SDSS that it was not feasible to attain a threshold of 40,000 students within a service distance of 100 km for each service center because of the underlying geographical distribution of student population in the state (Honey et al., 1991). The SDSS in this case produced maps of various service arrangements in addition to tables and other types of output.

One important implication of data collection issues for this type of geographical analysis of community organizations is that data must often be collected from numerous sources, even for a study in a relatively small target area involving few organizations (Foot, 1981, pp. 17-19). This increases the probability that the data will refer to different time periods, be reported for different aggregate spatial units, and be based on different operational definitions of variables. These inconsistencies in data are problematic. If data on the number of teachers were reported for 1990 but data on the numbers of students were reported for 1995, we could not develop an accurate teacher/student ratio for 1995. Several techniques are available for converting a set of data from one system of spatial units to another and for protecting confidentiality in dealing with spatially referenced data.

Areal interpolation refers to a set of techniques to estimate the distribution of a phenomenon across one set of spatial units (the source units) in terms of a second set of spatial units (the target units). A common approach to areal interpolation is the area-weighting method, which relies on the concept of map overlay (Lam, 1983). In this approach, a variable such as "total population for a census tract" is weighted by the proportion of the census tract's area that lies in the target unit. The resulting number of people is then assigned to the target unit as part of that unit's population (see Figure 2.11).

The areal interpolation can be enhanced by incorporating ancillary data (Flowerdew & Green, 1989). For example, if we know based on the distribution of streets or houses that no one actually lives in a certain part of the census tract, we can derive a better estimate of the population residing in the area of overlap between the two sets of spatial units (see Figure 2.12).

Mapping data poses particular confidentiality problems. For example, revealing that a particular individual was a female between the ages of 20 and 24 would probably not be sufficient information to reveal the identity of that person within a community. However, mapping the home location of a person will almost always be sufficient to identify a small group of individuals or, in some cases, a single individual. The spatial analysis can generally be conducted based on locations of individuals encoded in a database without actually mapping those locations. *To describe and report locational patterns to protect confidentiality, point locations, such as the locations of individual houses, can be randomly offset before they are mapped, or data can be aggregated to a set of areas (census blocks, towns) that are relevant to the research question.*

Definition: Areal interpolation involves using technques to estimate the distribution of a variable across one set of spatial units in terms of a second set

Key point

Figure 2.11.
Without additional information, we would estimate that about half of the total population of Census Tract 4977 lives in the target unit because about half of Tract 4977's area lies within the target unit.

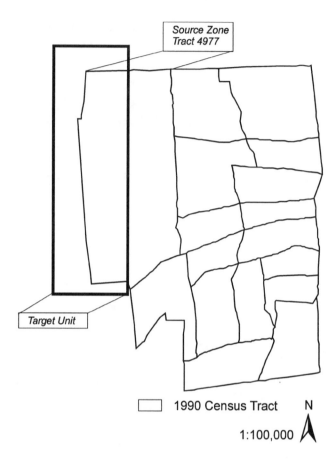

Source Zone
Tract 4977

Target Unit

☐ 1990 Census Tract   N

1:100,000 ⬆

SPATIAL SAMPLING

Community research that requires collecting data on how individuals and organizations function in a particular environment or how they perceive a particular environment usually entails sampling, because observing an entire population is too difficult and costly. In geographic terms, there are two main types of sampling: sampling *of* space and sampling *in* space (Goodchild, 1984, p. 47). **Sampling of space** is most appropriate when the variable being studied is continuous or observable everywhere over the earth's surface. Variables such as elevation or land cover or precipi-

Definition:
Sampling of space draws samples from all possible places in the study area

Figure 2.12.
Ancillary street
network data show
that not many
people live in the
target zone, and
the area-weighting
method of areal
interpolation would
probably over-
estimate the number
of people in the
target zone.

⟋⟍⟍ Street

☐ 1990 Census Tract   N

1:100,000 ▲

tation, which can be measured at any point on the land
surface, are usually measured by sampling in this way, at a
set of designated control points, because the set of all places
where these variables could be measured is infinite. When
the control points are laid out in a regular grid, the sampling
is systematic rather than random, and the sample will be
unbiased unless the variable being measured has marked
periodic properties.

Sampling in space involves drawing a sample from a
population of discrete objects (e.g., people, housing units,
or neighborhoods) that are themselves distributed across

Definition:
Sampling in
space draws a
sample from a
population of
discrete objects
or things arrayed
in space

the earth's surface. Sampling in space is a variant of the general sampling problem that involves selecting a sample from a population of discrete objects without regard to location. The concepts of random, systematic, and stratified sampling (see Books 1 and 2) can be evaluated for the case of sampling in space. A random sample of villagers will not be a random sample of all villagers in a settlement (the location in which they live) unless the villagers happen to be uniformly distributed within it. Placing a grid over a map and obtaining one case from each unit of the grid will yield a random sample of the set of all *places,* but it will probably not yield a random sample of the set of all *villagers.* Instead, we want to take a spatially stratified, random, or systematic sample of all villagers. Unfortunately for most community-based research, whereas the sampling frame for all places in the community is easy to determine from a map, the sampling frame of all villagers or households is more difficult to develop, and some type of cluster sampling strategy is often necessary.

EXAMPLE 2.6   ━▰━▰━▰━

DEVELOPING A SAMPLING FRAME FOR SPATIAL SAMPLING

In the case of the West Hartford school district, it would be difficult to obtain a list of all school-aged children in the Town of West Hartford (some of whom would not attend public school anyway), but it would be possible to perform cluster sampling by obtaining a list of all enrolled students from each school. A random or systematic sample could then be taken of the list provided by each school. If a neighborhood sent only a few children to school, however, it is likely that children from that neighborhood would not be adequately represented in the sample. In this instance, where the redistricting impacts would be variable by neighborhood yet of equal concern for every child regardless of the neighborhood where the child resided, we would need to take a spatially stratified random or systematic sample of each neighborhood in the town to ensure a representative sample.

━▰━▰━▰━

Because human beings are not uniformly distributed across the surface of the earth, and because we organize ourselves into households and communities with different social and economic characteristics, a sample of individuals from a population is implicitly a spatial sample. *Despite the* **Key point** *elaborate sampling schemes developed to produce representative samples, too little attention is explicitly paid to spatial sampling.* Given the high degree of residential segregation by class and race in many communities in the United States, any population sample by race is a spatial sample as well, because some racial groups live only in certain neighborhoods. If we see a correlation between race and low birth weight, for example, how can we be certain that race is not simply a surrogate measure for living in a particular part of town and being subjected to all of the environmental contaminants present there? *Meaningful* **Key point** *community-based research requires us to have an understanding of where individuals are located in the community and what parts of the community environment they use so that we can develop appropriate sampling schemes even when the ultimate object of the research is not spatial analysis per se.* A map can be a most useful tool for modeling the locations of individuals and organizations within a community.

MAPPING SPATIAL DATA

Maps as Models

Maps are models of the earth's surface. As models, maps are generalized representations of reality. Sophisticated map users realize that maps distort reality by simplifying the phenomena occurring on the complex, three-dimensional surface of the earth for representation on a flat sheet of paper or video screen. The "cartographic paradox" is that "to present a useful and truthful picture, an accurate map

Figure 2.13.
Different methods
for representing
map scale.

Ratio	1:24,000
Phrase	1 inch = 2,000 feet
Bar Graph	

must tell white lies" (Monmonier, 1996, p. 1). Scale, projection, and symbols are the three basic attributes of maps, and each is a source of distortion.

Definition:
Map scale
is the ratio
of map model
to reality

Map scale tells the user how much smaller the model is than the reality it represents. Map scale can be stated as a ratio, a phrase, or a simple bar graph. Ratio scales are particularly useful for map comparison (see Figure 2.13). A 1:5,000 map is a large-scale map (a map of a relatively small area showing high detail); a 1:1,000,000 is a small-scale map (a map of a large area showing limited detail). Graphic scales are particularly useful ways of representing scales on paper and digital maps because the scale will remain useful even if the map is enlarged or reduced during reproduction.

Scale is an important component of maps because scale affects the detail that can be represented. At the map scale in Figure 2.10, the locations of the schools in West Hartford can be represented. If the map had been drawn at a smaller scale, for example, a scale sufficient to depict the State of Connecticut on the page, the schools' locations could not be shown clearly. Most ethnographic research would involve the use of relatively large-scale maps of communities or settlements.

Definition:
Projection
transforms
curved earth
surface into flat
representation

Projection, a second basic component of maps, is the mathematical function that transforms locations from the curved, three-dimensional surface of the earth to a flat, two-dimensional representation (Pearson, 1990). This process can distort map scale significantly. *Although scale can be constant at all points and in all directions on a globe as a true scale model of the earth, scale varies from point to point*

Key point

Unprojected

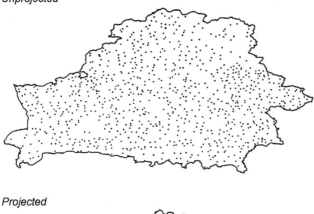

Figure 2.14. The impact of map projection is demonstrated by displaying the view of the unprojected boundary of Belarus and the view of the projected boundary of Belarus.

Projected

and with direction from a point on a paper map because flat maps stretch some distances and shrink others. Choice of map projection affects other spatial relationships represented in a map, including direction and sizes and shapes of areas (see Figure 2.14).

Map projection is probably a more serious issue for users of small-scale maps and projected digital spatial databases. Paper maps of small areas, which are the kinds of maps that many ethnographers would likely use, would not be as seriously affected by choice of map projection as would maps of the world or continental land masses prepared using different map projections. Nevertheless, map projections have certainly influenced cultural perceptions of size, shape, and orientation of land surfaces (Monmonier, 1996, pp. 97-99).

Symbols are used to represent objects on the earth's surface as points, lines, and areas. Topographic maps are used to depict the surface configuration. They indicate changes in elevation and the locations of objects such as surface water features, roads, and structures. These maps are useful for wayfinding and locating places. Topographic map coverage is available for most countries of the world at scales generally ranging from 1:24,000 to 1:100,000. Maps of this type often rely on standardized symbologies.

Another common type of map developed over the past two centuries is the statistical map. These maps are a kind of statistical graphic intended to show the distribution of a variable in geographical space (Tufte, 1983). Most statistical maps rely on a single type of symbol, such as a dot, to represent population (see Figure 2.15).

Monmonier (1996, p. 20) identifies six dimensions of visual variability of map symbols: size, shape, value, texture, orientation, and hue. These aspects of symbolization can be and are manipulated to achieve certain objectives in cartographic communication (see Figure 2.16). Standard cartography texts provide useful guidelines for map compilation and design, and one body of cartographic research evaluates the impact of different symbolizations on the perceptions of map users (MacEachern, 1994).

Geographic Information Systems

Cartography and spatial database management have been profoundly influenced by the development of computers (Dobson, 1983). Computer-assisted cartography en-

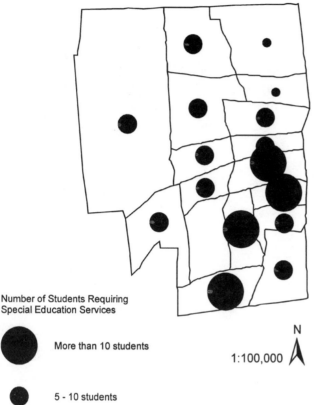

Figure 2.15.
A statistical map using graduated circles to depict the distribution of students requiring special education services by census tract.

Number of Students Requiring
Special Education Services

 More than 10 students

1:100,000 N ⤒

 5 - 10 students

● Fewer than 5 students

ables a separation of the data storage and data display functions that are completely integrated in the paper map. This makes it possible to produce many different kinds of displays from the same databases relatively quickly. Computer cartography also made it possible to separate the geographic data (the locations of points, lines, and areas) from the thematic data (the attributes of the points, lines, and areas). If we have a database of census tract boundaries, for example, stored separately from a database of census tract populations, we can change the population without

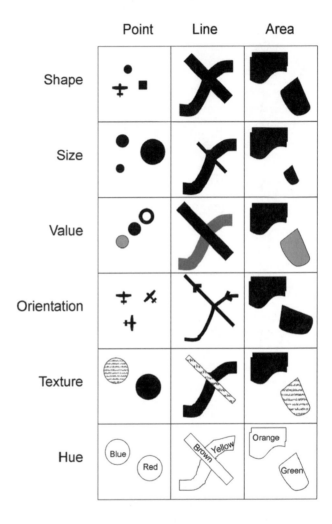

Figure 2.16.
Six dimensions of
variability in map
symbols.
SOURCE: Adapted
from Monmonier
(1996).

having to reproduce the entire map by hand. Computer cartography has also made it possible to produce displays such as three-dimensional maps, which are often extremely difficult to produce by hand.

Over the past several decades, advances in computer hardware, graphics software, and database management systems have come together in geographic information systems.

Geographic information systems (GISs) (Maguire, Goodchild, & Rhind, 1991) use computer software that supports three main functions: spatial database management, visualization and mapping, and spatial analysis. As a result, GIS software systems are more powerful than computer graphics or mapping software. GISs can provide the multiple views of data—tabular, graphic, and statistical—described in Figures 2.1 and 2.2.

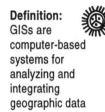

Definition: GISs are computer-based systems for analyzing and integrating geographic data

In response to this developing technology, the government agencies that are traditionally responsible for map production in the United States and other countries have created digital spatial databases containing the same kinds of information found on topographic maps. Many of these databases are available via the Internet, and commercial vendors have entered the market to upgrade and customize databases to meet particular user needs. In fact, GIS technology is now being used to produce and manage most of the spatial data compiled by government agencies at all levels in the United States and internationally.

"Map" information is increasingly being delivered in the form of a digital database rather than a paper map, and users of these maps will need to have some level of GIS expertise to obtain the information formerly provided on paper maps. The GIS industry today is a global industry with hundreds of software database products (Rodkay, 1995). Hardware and software developments have made it possible now to develop GIS applications on laptop computers. This enables a high level of mapmaking in both the research laboratory and the field.

Maps and spatial databases can be incorporated into many phases of ethnographic research. Prior to fieldwork, maps may be used for study area or sample selection. During research, maps may be used for wayfinding and data collection. Finally, maps can provide a method for analysis in addition to spatial statistical analysis and are useful for

Figure 2.17.
Regular tesselations
associated with the
field model of space.

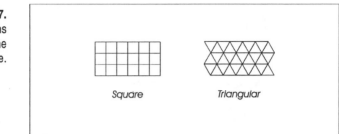

Figure 2.17. Regular tesselations associated with the field model of space.

Square   Triangular

reporting the results of community-based research. The primary requirement for mapping or spatial database development is that objects of interest can be located on the earth's surface.

Operationalizing Location

Spatial analysis requires us to describe the locations of the people and organizations that we are studying. Location means position in space. When we think about the earth's surface as a geographic space, there are two fundamental approaches to modeling it. On one hand, we can subdivide the surface into a set of conformal equal-area units, units of the same size and shape, called a *regular tesselation*. We can

 Definition: The field model identifies equal units of space and assigns attributes to them

then assign attributes to these locations (land cover, soil type, etc.; see Figure 2.17). This model of space, the **field model,** helps us to represent "what is everywhere" (Worboys, 1995). Very often, the kinds of features modeled in this way represent features that are continuously distributed across the earth's surface. On the other hand, we can

 Definition: The object model identifies objects of interest and assigns them to a space

identify objects of interest (people, farms, schools) and position these objects in an otherwise empty space (see Figure 2.18). This model of space, the **object model,** helps us to represent "where everything is." This model is useful when the features modeled are discrete. *The units of analysis*

 Key point

in most ethnographic research will be discrete from a geographic point of view.

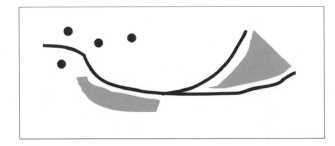

Figure 2.18. Points, lines, and areas associated with the object model of space.

Geocoding is "the process by which an entity on the earth's surface, a household, for example, is given a label identifying its location with respect to some common point or frame of reference" (Goodchild, 1984, p. 33). There are two main approaches to describing the position of an object in space. *Absolute location* describes the position of an object with respect to an arbitrary grid system such as latitude/longitude, *state plane coordinates,* or a coordinate system devised by the researcher. The state plane coordinate system in the United States is a coordinate system based on zones drawn state by state on transverse Mercator or Lambert conformal projections (Pearson, 1990). The absolute location states the position of a point in such terms that the point's unique position with respect to all other points on the earth is clear. "West Hartford town center is 41.45N and 72.45W" is a statement of absolute location. *Relative location* describes the position of an object with respect to other objects in the geographic space. "West Hartford is the town immediately west of Hartford" and "West Hartford is a 60-minute drive from New York City" are statements of relative location.

In conducting research on travel and activity patterns, the ethnographer can make lists of places where respondents live and engage in other activities (Tom's house, 20 Beverly Road, Whiting Lane School). As noted earlier, these lists or tables do not generally preserve or reveal the spatial arrangements of activity sites. To map the activity sites,

Definition: Geocoding involves giving an entity on the earth's surface a spatial designation or label

there must be some way to convert "Tom's house" to its location on the earth's surface.

Absolute location can be measured directly from the earth's surface by surveying (McCormac, 1995). With the development of satellite technology, we can now use global positioning systems (GPS) to ascertain absolute locations on the earth's surface (Van Sickle, 1996). Latitude/longitude geocodes that have been determined for particular places are also sometimes published in gazetteers or other archival sources (e.g., see Abate, 1991).

More commonly, absolute location is estimated from an existing model of space that has been created at a particular scale. For example, we could estimate the latitude/longitude location of a school by taking it off an appropriately anno-tated topographic map. We could also estimate the lati-tude/longitude of a school by using a GIS to address-match geocode an address against a digital, address-ranged street network (Drummond, 1995).

Digital images are also available to aid location. Digital orthophotos are photos of portions of the earth's surface taken from satellite images. These images are available at scales that enable identification of landscape features such as buildings and roads (see Figure 2.19).

Because GISs enable integration of spatial databases from different sources compiled at different scales, intelli-gent users of spatial data need to be sensitive to the issue of error in spatial databases (Goodchild & Gopal, 1989). As the discussion on maps indicates, spatial data are inherently inaccurate. Even a location estimated using GPS may be accurate within several meters at best. The error issue is complicated by digital processing of spatial data. The pre-cision with which computer mapping and GIS software can calculate distances, areas, and other spatial attributes is much greater than the underlying accuracy of the location measurement. As spatial databases are combined within

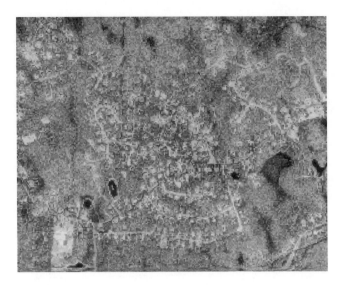

Figure 2.19.
A portion of a digital orthophotoquad featuring a residential neighborhood in Connecticut.

GIS to create new databases, error propagates through the stages of the analysis.

Depending upon the research application, absolute map accuracy may not be paramount. Instead, it may be important to capture only accurate *relative* locations of activity sites within the study area. Regardless, researchers should be aware of the level of error present within the spatial databases used in the research project and select analytical procedures that are tolerant of that level of error.

Most ethnographic research brings the researcher into the community. As a consequence, there will be an opportunity for direct observation of the environment and assessment of error in available spatial databases. Large-scale map and digital database coverage varies widely from place to place, and few large-scale maps may be available for the study area of interest. The Suggested Resources section provides a brief summary of sources of maps and digital spatial data. For those communities for which no appropriate cartographic base is available, researchers can develop their own cartographic representations.

Figure 2.20.
Activity space for a
single child showing
the home base and
trips made during
one week to other
activity sites,
including school,
church, and a
shopping center.

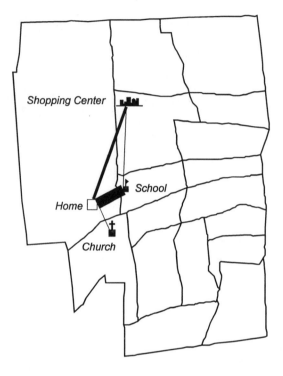

Figure 2.20. Activity space for a single child showing the home base and trips made during one week to other activity sites, including school, church, and a shopping center.

Mapping home locations and activity sites. In the same way that anthropologists and other social scientists have examined gross time allocation, geographers have mapped the allocation of individuals to space. We are familiar with many of these maps, yet rarely think of them in terms of the time-space patterns of individuals that underlie them. It is relatively easy to map the activity space (show the locations) for a single individual, even over a long period of time. Displaying the activity spaces (showing the multiple locations) of many individuals often results in a map that is illegible (see Figures 2.20 and 2.21).

A common response to this problem is to limit the number of activity sites that are represented for each individual and to aggregate the sites spatially. The most obvious example is the map of population distribution based on residential location, the home location having been selected

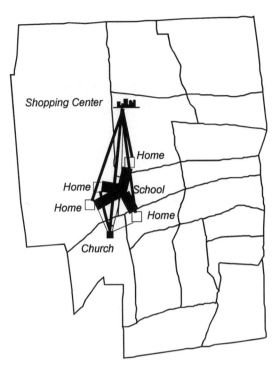

Figure 2.21.
Representing activity spaces for more than one child produces a map that is difficult to interpret.

by virtue of its importance as a node in the individual's activity space. Although time and space can both be measured continuously, time allocation studies often convert a continuous variable such as time into discrete units of a variable by observing activities at particular time intervals. A number of approaches have been taken to aggregating population data for mapping purposes: the dot density map, the graduated circle map, and the choropleth map (see Figure 2.22).

Location can also be measured continuously, as when analysts assign a latitude/longitude geocode to an individual engaged in a particular activity. Until the introduction of computer-assisted cartography, it was very difficult to compile a map that stored and displayed the locations of many individuals in continuous space at a reasonable scale. The two main analytical approaches to representing this

Definition:
A choropleth map displays areally based data thematically by tonal shading proportional to the density of area units

Figure 2.22.
Representing the
same population
data using dot
density, graduated
symbol, and
choropleth maps.

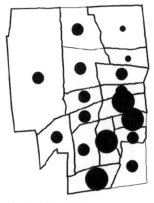

Dot Density

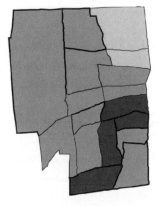

Graduated Symbol

Choropleth

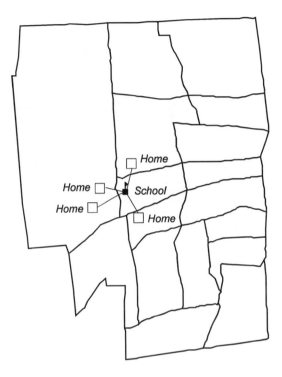

Figure 2.23.
Mapping trips from
many origins
to a single activity
site—the journey
to school.

complexity have been the following: (a) grid cell techniques (often used with associated travel vectors); and (b) centrographic techniques, such as the mean center, standard distance, and standard deviational ellipse (Ebdon, 1977).

Taking a different approach, some activity maps simplify by examining the relationships between home location and other destinations where only one kind of activity (work, school, shopping, receiving medical care) takes place (see Figure 2.23). Beyond this, representation of the activity space becomes more difficult. Some analysts have identified a set of locations or divided space into a set of geographic "intervals" or areas (by superimposing a grid) and then measured the number of times individuals are found at those points or in those intervals (see Figure 2.24). This approach is useful when the analyst wishes to evaluate how many people will be affected by changes in the local envi-

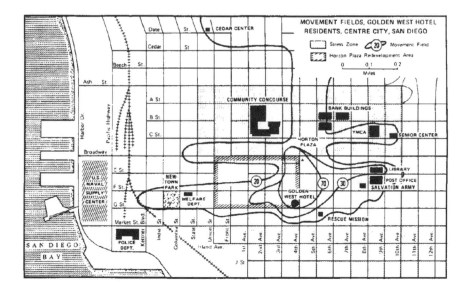

Figure 2.24.
Mapping activity
patterns by showing
the proportion of
people who would
be likely to visit
those areas over a
period of 1 week.
SOURCE: Stutz
(1976). Used by
permission of the
American
Geographical
Society.

ronment, not because the place that is being changed is where they live but because the place is a place they visit regularly in their travel and activity patterns (Stutz, 1976).

Map comparison. Travel and activity patterns are often analyzed for groups of individuals defined beforehand by one or more characteristics, such as age and sex or neighborhood of residence. For example, time allocation patterns for women and men are often compared. An alternative approach to analyzing individual travel and activity patterns enables researchers to group individuals based on similarity of travel and activity patterns.

One approach to this problem would be to prepare maps of individual activity spaces and attempt an assessment of similarity by visual comparison. Visual map comparison, a basic and often effective research method, is facilitated by a GIS, which makes cartographic overlay of maps very easy provided that the maps can be depicted at the same scale, using the same projection and the same origin. The most important drawback to this approach is that not everyone will perceive the same degree of areal association among the distributions being compared.

Some numerical measures are available for evaluating similarities of geographical distributions. In its earliest application, one similarity measure that can be modified for this purpose was used to track the behavior of individual animals in migrating herds (Cole, 1949; Lehner, 1979). The similarity measure was later adapted to analyze the activity spaces of elderly residents of Flint, Michigan, who recalled destinations regularly visited for work, shopping, recreation, medical care, and other activities (Cromley & Shannon, 1986). This similarity measure compared the total number of times that two individuals were observed in the same place to the total number of times that both individuals were observed. It is possible to extend this model to compare the total number of times that two individuals are observed at the same place, at the same time, engaging in the same activity to the total number of times that both individuals are observed.

$$I_{ab} = 2ab/(a + b)$$

where

   I_{ab} = index of similarity value for individuals A and B
   ab = total number of observations for which individuals
        A and B are in the same place, at the same time, and
        engaged in the same activity
   a = total number of observations of Person A
   b = total number of observations of Person B

The value of the index varies linearly from 0.0 (no correspondence in activity patterns) to 1.0 (perfect correspondence of activity patterns in time and space) when a and b are constant as the number of matching activities increases. High index values identify respondent pairs with similar activity patterns; low index values identify respondent pairs with different activity patterns. If home location is included as an activity site, perfect correspondence can be achieved only for the activities spaces of individuals who share a home location. It is possible to adapt the similarity measure for different research purposes by dropping home location as an observation point, for example, to identify people whose activity spaces are the same when they are not at home.

This measure can be used based on place alone, without involving maps. That is, we can develop similarity measures based on reported names of places or street addresses even if the latitude/longitude locations of those places were not known. We could not, however, develop cartographic representations of the individual and shared activity spaces without being able to locate the activity sites on a model of the earth's surface.

When we have mapped the locations where people spend time, either as points or areas, numerical measures of map correspondence can be applied. Minnick's (1964) coefficient of areal correspondence (or C_a) is similar to the measure described above and is calculated using the formula below:

$$C_a = \frac{\text{places or areas over which phenomena are located together}}{\text{total places or area covered by both phenomena}}$$

Once groups of respondents who have similar travel and activity patterns have been identified, it is relatively easy to map the set of locations that they visit in common. It is also possible to analyze other attributes of groups of individuals who share common activity spaces. The researcher can identify, for example, activity patterns associated only with particular age, sex, ethnic, or residential neighborhood groups and activity patterns that are not associated with other characteristics of group members.

These geographical dimensions of activity space similarity/dissimilarity can be meaningfully explored by multidimensional scaling. Multidimensional scaling is a procedure that assigns numbers to various quantities of attributes of the phenomena being scaled such that the numbers directly reflect variations in the quantities of the attributes among the phenomena being scaled (Golledge & Rushton, 1972). Objects (in this case, the activity spaces being scaled) are likely to vary with respect to the number of activity locations, dispersion of activity locations, and other attributes. These attributes form a multidimensional series, and the scaling procedure is designed to identify a number of relevant dimensions of the activity spaces. The quantity of each attribute associated with a given object can then be interpreted as a coordinate that, when used in conjunction with the coordinates of other attributes, determines the location of each object in the multidimensional attribute space. Greater degrees of similarity in the original data result in smaller distances in the attribute space, and lesser degrees of similarity are associated with greater distances in the attribute space.

The chief input required for multidimensional scaling is a set of proximity measures such as measures of similarity or dissimilarity that may be metric or nonmetric (Kruskal, Young, & Seery, 1976). A *proximity matrix* is created by listing every unit of observation as a row and as a column of the matrix and then recording the similarity of every observation with every other observation in the cells of the matrix. The aim of multidimensional scaling is to take the proximity matrix and convert the measured dissimilarities into explicit distances along a set of dimensions identified by the scaling procedure. In effect, multidimensional scaling enables a remapping of space. In using multidimensional scaling to explore similarities and differences in in-

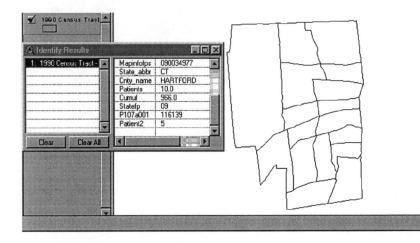

Figure 2.25.
Accessing a table and a map representing the same data using a geographic information system.

dividuals' activity spaces, we can group individuals into new "neighborhoods" based not solely on residential location but on their total use of the environment. Multidimensional scaling has also been used to evaluate dimensions in individuals' mental maps of their living environments (Golledge, Rivizzigno, & Spector, 1976).

The various data collection and analytical approaches described in the preceding sections involve spatially referenced data. As such, the data and output of the analyses can be mapped in most cases, although the data *need not* be mapped. As shown in Figure 2.25, mapping and numerical analysis provide alternative but complementary views of the data, and multiple views of data are necessary to provide a complete picture of the community at hand. The use of maps to describe data is constrained by confidentiality issues in a way that reporting summary statistics may not be. Regardless, the aim of mapping and numerical analyses is to provide a richer understanding of how communities work in real and imagined geographic space, perhaps as an aid to solving problems within communities.

THE POWER OF MAPS

Maps are recognized as one of the main categories of cultural materials available for ethnographic research (Murdock, 1971). Maps are tremendous stores of data—consider how long it would take to describe verbally all of the information on even a simple statistical map. Maps also provide alternative views or visualizations of data from the views offered by tabular presentation or statistical analysis. As such, maps can be an important component of ethnographic research.

Effective map interpretation and map-making requires skill, however. Although often viewed as precise portrayals of the earth's surface, maps are necessarily distorted models of the reality they represent. An understanding of how maps work is perhaps more important than ever given the explosion of spatial databases and computer-based systems for analyzing them.

That map-making is no longer solely in the hands of expert cartographers (if it ever was) is not necessarily a cause for concern (Wood, 1992). Maps are not neutral. They promote specific interests, and there is no reason why the interests and viewpoints of ethnographers should not be explored through maps.

Nevertheless, care must taken to consider the extent to which maps produced as an aid to ethnographic research might harm community members. One potential source of harm is revealing confidential information. Another potential source of harm is alerting individuals to problems that they cannot address. For example, producing a map of environmental contamination within a community can have serious psychological and health implications for residents who live within a contaminated zone but do not have the means to leave or eliminate the contamination.

An important ethical standard for research involving human subjects is that people participating in research projects should enjoy the benefits of the research and that the results of the research should not be withheld. Given that map-making and spatial data compilation and analysis are increasingly accomplished through computer-assisted means, researchers using these methods need to think about how they can and should share the research with community members. Some spatial databases sold by vendors cannot be distributed freely. GIS software, like other software, may be subject to licensing requirements that prevent copying. Communities may not have access to the hardware, software, and databases necessary to use the spatial data or analytical procedures that the ethnographer has used. Concerns about GIS as a means of surveillance and control merit serious consideration (Pickles, 1995). There have also been efforts to develop community-based geographic information systems so that maps reflecting the interests of community groups can be developed as counterpoints to the maps offered by government agencies, corporations, and planners.

A more subtle issue in the use of maps for ethnographic research is their contribution to a spatial fallacy. Everything that occurs on the surface of the earth can be mapped. That is, we can map almost anything, but mapping does not necessarily create meaning. Maps, because of their visual power, often become metaphors for the social relationships and problems that are contained in geographic space. This makes it tempting to look for spatial solutions to problems. Although many social problems have a spatial dimension— and some issues in society can be addressed by changing locational relationships, such as drawing new school district boundaries—mapping may not be an aid to analysis for other problems. Even for problems that have a strong spatial dimension, changes in spatial organization often contribute to the emergence of new locational conflicts.

With these caveats, the role of maps in ethnographic research is potentially great. Maps are important for describing study areas, collecting and analyzing data, and reporting results. As computer technology continues to transform our spatial data handling and mapping capabilities, new roles for mapping in ethnographic research may emerge. The tools for exploring the spatial dimensions of community life will continue to be an essential part of the ethnographer's toolkit.

REFERENCES

Abate, F. R. (1991). *Omni gazetteer of the United States of America.* Detroit, MI: Omnigraphics.

Aitken, S. C. (1994). *Putting children in their place.* Washington, DC: Association of American Geographers.

Alter, C. F. (1988). The changing structure of elderly service delivery systems. *The Gerontologist, 28,* 91-98.

Anderson, J. (1971). Space-time budgets and activity studies in urban geography and planning. *Environment and Planning, 3,* 353-368.

Anscombe, F. J. (1973). Graphs in statistical analysis. *American Statistician, 27,* 17-21.

Bailey, T. C., & Gatrell, A. C. (1995). *Interactive spatial data analysis.* Essex, UK: Longman Scientific & Technical.

Bernard, H. R. (1995). *Research methods in anthropology* (2nd ed.). Walnut Creek, CA: AltaMira.

Bernard, H. R., & Killworth, P. D. (1993). Sampling in time allocation research. *Ethnology, 32,* 207-215.

Bernard, H. R., Killworth, P., Kronfeld, D., & Sailor, L. (1984). The problem of informant accuracy: The validity of retrospective data. *Annual Review of Anthropology, 13,* 495-517.

Brakel, S., Parry, J., & Weiner, B. (1985). *The mentally disabled and the law.* Chicago: American Bar Association.

Carlstein, T. (1982). *Time resources, society and ecology.* London: Allen and Unwin.

Christaller, W. (1966). *Central places in southern Germany* (C. W. Baskin, Trans.). Englewood Cliffs, NJ: Prentice Hall. (Originally published in 1933)

Cohen, R. J., Haddix, K., Hurtado, E., & Dewey, K. G. (1995). Maternal activity budgets: Feasibility of exclusive breastfeeding for six months among urban women in Honduras. *Social Science and Medicine, 41,* 527-536.

Cole, L. C. (1949). The measurement of interspecific association. *Ecology, 30,* 411-424.

Cromley, E. K., & Shannon, G. W. (1986). Locating ambulatory medical care facilities for the elderly. *Health Services Research, 21,* 499-514.

Department of Education, State of Connecticut. (1994). *Connecticut education directory, 1994-95.* Hartford: State of Connecticut.

Dobson, J. E. (1983). Automated geography. *The Professional Geographer, 35,* 135-143.

Drummond, W. J. (1995). Address matching: GIS technology for mapping human activity patterns. *Journal of American Planning Association, 61,* 240-251.

Dyck, I. (1990). Space, time and renegotiating motherhood: An exploration of the domestic workplace. *Environment and Planning D, 8,* 459-483.

Ebdon, D. (1977). *Statistics in geography: A practical approach.* Oxford, UK: Basil Blackwell.

Edmundson, W. C. (1976). *Land, food and work in East Java.* Armidale, Australia: University of New England Press.

Eyles, J. (1985). *Sense of place.* Warrington, UK: Silverbrook.

Flowerdew, R., & Green, M. (1989). Statistical methods for inference between incompatible zonal systems. In M. F. Goodchild & S. Gopal (Eds.), *Accuracy of spatial databases* (pp. 239-248). London: Taylor and Francis.

Foot, D. (1981). *Operational urban models.* London: Methuen.

Fuchs, V. R. (Ed.). (1996). *Individual and social responsibility: Child care, education, medical care, and long-term care in America.* Chicago: University of Chicago Press.

Gans, S. P., & Horton, G. T. (1975). *Integration of human services: The state and municipal levels.* New York: Praeger.

Garling, T., Book, A., & Lindberg, E. (1979). The acquisition and use of an internal representation of the spatial layout of the environment during locomotion. *Man-Environment Systems, 9,* 200-208.

Gatrell, A. (1983). *Distance and space.* Oxford, UK: Clarendon.

Ghosh, A., & Rushton, G. (Eds.). (1987). *Spatial analysis and location-allocation models.* New York: Van Nostrand Reinhold.

Golledge, R. G., & Brown, L. A. (1967). Search, learning and the market decision process. *Geografiska Annaler, 49B,* 116-124.

Golledge, R. G., Rivizzigno, V. L., & Spector, A. (1976). Learning about a city: Analysis by multidimensional scaling. In R. G. Golledge & G. Rushton (Eds.), *Spatial choice and spatial behavior* (pp. 95-116). Columbus: Ohio State University Press.

Golledge, R. G., & Rushton, G. (1972). *Multidimensional scaling: Review and geographical applications* (Commission on College Geography Technical Paper No. 10). Washington, DC: Association of American Geographers.

Golledge, R. G., & Stimson, R. J. (1987). *Analytical behavioural geography.* London: Croom Helm.

Golledge, R. G., & Stimson, R. J. (1997). *Spatial behavior: A geographic perspective.* New York: Guilford.

Goodchild, M. F. (1984). Geocoding and geosampling. In G. L. Gaile & C. J. Willmott (Eds.), *Spatial statistics and models* (pp. 33-53). Dordrecht: D. Reidel.

Goodchild, M. F., & Gopal, S. (Eds.). (1989). *Accuracy of spatial databases.* London: Taylor and Francis.

Grossman, L. S. (1984). Collecting time-use data in Third World rural communities. *The Professional Geographer, 36,* 444-454.

Gulick, J. (1966). Images of an Arab city. *Journal of the American Institute of Planners, 29,* 179-197.

Hagerstrand, T. (1970). What about people in regional science? *Papers and Proceedings of the Regional Science Association, 25,* 7-21.

Hall, E. T. (1966). *The hidden dimension.* Garden City, NY: Doubleday.

Hensher, D., & Stopher, P. (1979). *Behavioural travel demand modelling.* London: Croom Helm.

Honey, R., Rushton, G., Lolonis, P., Dalziel, B. T., Armstrong, M. P., De, S., & Densham, P. J. (1991). Stages in the adoption of a spatial decision support system for reorganizing service delivery regions. *Environment and Planning C: Government and Policy, 9,* 51-63.

Jakle, J. A., Brunn, S., & Roseman, C. C. (1976). *Human spatial behavior: A social geography.* North Scituate, MA: Duxbury.

Johnson, A. (1975). Time allocation in a Machiguenga community. *Ethnology, 14,* 301-310.

Johnston, R. J., Gregory, D., & Smith, D. M. (Eds.). (1994). *The dictionary of human geography* (3rd ed.). Oxford, UK: Basil Blackwell.

Jones, P. M. (1979). HATS: A technique for investigating household decisions. *Environment and Planning A, 11,* 59-70.

Kruskal, J. B., Young, F. W., & Seery, J. B. (1976). *How to use KYST-2, a very flexible program to do multidimensional scaling and unfolding.* Murray Hill, NJ: Bell Labs.

Lam, N. S. (1983). Spatial interpolation methods: A review. *American Cartographer, 10,* 129-149.

LeCompte, M. D., & Preissle, J. (1993). *Ethnography and qualitative design in educational research.* San Diego, CA: Academic Press.

Lehner, P. N. (1979). *Handbook of ethological methods.* New York: Garland STPM Press.

Levinson, D., & Kumar, A. (1995). Activity, travel, and the allocation of time. *Journal of the American Planning Association, 61,* 458-470.

Ley, D. (1989). Modernism, post-modernism and the struggle for place. In J. Agnes & J. Duncan (Eds.), *The power of place: Bringing together the geographical and sociological imaginations* (pp. 44-65). London: Unwin Hyman.

Lynch, K. (1960). *The image of the city.* Cambridge: MIT Press.

MacEachern, A. M. (1994). *Some truth with maps: A primer on symbolization and design.* Washington, DC: Association of American Geographers.

Maguire, D. J., Goodchild, M. F., & Rhind, D. W. (Eds.). (1991). *Geographical information systems: Principles and applications.* Harlow, UK: Longman Scientific and Technical.

Malczewski, J., & Orgyczak, W. (1995). The multiple criteria location problem: 1. A generalized network model and the set of efficient solutions. *Environment and Planning A, 27,* 1931-1960.

Malczewski, J., & Orgyczak, W. (1996). The multiple criteria location problem: 2. Preference-based techniques and interactive decision support. *Environment and Planning A, 28,* 69-98.

McCormac, J. C. (1995). *Surveying* (3rd ed.). Englewood Cliffs, NJ: Prentice Hall.

Minnick, R. F. (1964). A method for the measurement of areal correspondence. *Papers of the Michigan Academy of Science, Arts and Letters, 49,* 333-344.

Monmonier, M. (1996). *How to lie with maps* (2nd ed.). Chicago: University of Chicago Press.

Murdock, G. P. (1971). *Outline of cultural materials* (4th rev. ed.). New Haven, CT: Human Relations Area Files.

Oppong, J. R. (1996). Accommodating the rainy season in Third World location-allocation applications. *Socio-Economic Planning Sciences, 30,* 121-137.

Orleans, P., & Schmidt, S. (1972). Mapping the city: Environmental cognition of urban residents. In W. J. Mitchel (Ed.), *Environmental design: Research and practice* (pp. 1.4.1-1.4.9). Proceedings of the ERDA 3/AR8 Conference, University of California, Los Angeles.

Pearson, F., II. (1990). *Map projections: Theory and applications.* Boca Raton, FL: CRC Press.

Penchansky, R., & Thomas, W. J. (1981). The concept of access: Definition and relationships to consumer satisfaction. *Medical Care, 19,* 127-140.

Piaget, J., & Inhelder, B. (1967). *The child's conception of space.* New York: Norton.

Pickles, J. (1995). *Ground truth: The social implications of geographic information systems.* New York: Guilford.

Rabin, J., & Steinhauer, M. B. (Eds.). (1988). *Handbook on human services administration.* New York: Marcel Dekker.

Ricci, J. A., Jerome, N. W., Megally, N., Galal, O., Harrison, G. G., & Kirksey, A. (1995). Assessing the validity of informant recall: Results of a time use pilot study in peri-urban Egypt. *Human Organization, 54,* 304-308.

Rocha, J. (1994, October 10). School districts track gate-crashers: Nonresident students are targeted. *Hartford Courant,* 6 Hartford South Final, p. B1.

Rodkay, G. K. (Ed.). (1995). *GIS World sourcebook 1996.* Fort Collins, CO: GIS World.

Rowles, G. D. (1986). The geography of ageing and the aged: Towards an integrated perspective. *Progress in Human Geography, 10,* 511-540.

Ruddle, K. (1974). *The Yukpa cultivation system: A study of shifting cultivation in Colombia and Venezuela.* Berkeley: University of California Press.

Rugg, D. J., & Buech, R. R. (1990). Analyzing time budgets with Markov chains. *Biometrics, 46,* 1123-1131.

Rushton, G. (1984). Use of location-allocation models for improving geographical accessibility of rural services in developing countries. *International Regional Science Review, 9,* 217-240.

Rushton, G. (1988). Location theory, location-allocation models and service development planning in the Third World. *Economic Geography, 64,* 97-120.

Siegel, A. W. (1981). The externalization of cognitive maps by children and adults: In search of better ways to ask better questions. In L. S. Liben, A. Patterson, & N. Newcombe (Eds.), *Spatial representation and behavior across the life span* (pp. 167-194). New York: Academic Press.

Smith, N. J. H. (1981). *Man, fishers, and the Amazon.* New York: Columbia University Press.

Stutz, F. P. (1976). Adjustment and mobility of elderly poor and downtown renewal. *Geographical Review, 66,* 391-400.

Trotta, B. M. (1994, July 6). Board sets deadline for reorganizing elementary schools. *Hartford Courant,* 5E West Hartford Farmington Valley, p. D3.

Tufte, E. J. (1983). *The visual display of quantitative information.* Cheshire, CT: Graphics Press.

Tuma, N. J., & Hannan, M. T. (1984). *Social dynamics: Models and methods.* Orlando, FL: Academic Press.

Van Sickle, J. (1996). *GPS for land surveyors.* Chelsea, MI: Ann Arbor Press.

Wood, D. (1992). *The power of maps.* New York: Guilford.

Worboys, M. F. (1995). *GIS: A computing perspective.* Bristol, PA: Taylor & Francis.

SUGGESTED RESOURCES

A number of reference sources provide points of contact for acquiring maps and spatial databases that might be of use in ethnographic research.

Warnecke, L., Johnson, J. M., Marshall, K., & Brown, R. S. (1992). *State geographical information activities compendium.* Lexington, KY: Council of State Governments.

Mapping and spatial database development activities are becoming more decentralized within the United States. This reference provides a useful guide to map and spatial data sources for researchers working in particular states of the United States.

Böhme, R. (Ed.). (1989). *Inventory of world topographic mapping, Vols. 1-3.* London: Elsevier Applied Science.

This reference tool describes topographic maps series by country around the world. The scale of mapping and coverage are reported.

Armstrong, C. J. (Ed.). (1995). *World databases in geography and geology.* London: Bowker Saur.

This reference publication provides a description of the database, including its contents, start year, update schedule, downloading charges, and media. It also contains citations for published reviews of the databases.

Dubreuil, L. (Ed.). (1993). *World directory of map collections* (3rd ed.). International Federation of Library Associations and Institutions IFLA Publications 63. Munich: K. G. Saur.

This reference tool identifies libraries and institutions around the world that maintain map collections. For each institution, a standard set of data is provided, including person in charge; date of map collection establishment; number of staff; area occupied by collection; scale of coverage; special collections; control (cataloging system, etc.); access (hours, etc.); lending policies; and copying facilities.

Changes in the world political situation have made it much easier to purchase map products from around the world. The former Soviet Union, for example, was relatively closed as far as cartographic products were concerned. Now, maps produced during the Soviet era of the Soviet Union and many other countries in the world are available. The researcher may wish to contact the following companies for copies of their catalogues and additional information about products and services:

GeoCenter ILH
Internationales Landkartenhaus
Schockenriedstraße 44, D-70565 Stuttgart
Postal Address: Post Box 80 08 30, D-70508 Stuttgart, Germany
Telephone: (0711) 7 88 93 40
Fax: (0711) 7 88 93 54

Map Link Inc.
25 East Mason Street
Santa Barbara, CA 93101
USA
Telephone: (805) 965-4402
Free Fax: (800) 627-7768

Omni Resources
1004 South Mebane Street
P.O. Box 2096
Burlington, NC 27216
USA
Telephone: (910) 229-OMNI
Fax: (800) 449-OMNI

3 ━●━●━●━

STUDYING HIDDEN POPULATIONS

Merrill Singer

What Are Hidden Populations?
•
Evolution of Hidden Population Research
•
Recruiting Study Participants
•
Methodological Considerations
•
Ethical Issues
•
Conclusions

WHAT ARE HIDDEN POPULATIONS?

The recent reemergence of infectious disease as a major health issue in developed countries brings into bold relief the fundamental importance of learning about populations that are hard to find, hard to retain in intervention, and hard to relocate for follow-up assessment. In an epidemic, what have come to be called "hidden populations"—groups that reside outside of institutional and clinical settings and whose "activities are clandestine and therefore concealed from the view of mainstream society and agencies of social control" (Watters & Biernacki, 1989, p. 417), as well as from local community-based organizations—may be at special risk for infection and for transmitting infection to other populations. However, lack of knowledge about these groups hampers intervention strategies, and intentional or inadvertent concealment makes it difficult to reach them with targeted services. An example is seen in the following case (Singer & Marxuach-Rodriquez, 1996).

EXAMPLE 3.1   ━●━●━●━

IMPORTANCE OF RESEARCH IN SERVING HIDDEN POPULATIONS

In 1991, the Hispanic Health Council, a community-based health research and service organization in Hartford, Connecticut, was funded through the Northeast Hispanic AIDS Consortium to implement an AIDS prevention project targeted to Latino men who have sex with men (MSM). This initiative was launched because it was recognized that despite higher rates of HIV infection among minority MSM compared to their straight counterparts, many Latino MSM are not involved in existing AIDS prevention programs targeted to gay men in the city. In fact, many Latino MSM do not identify themselves as "gay" even if all of their sex partners are male because they feel that this label would diminish their ethnic heritage. Consequently, Latino MSM were less well known than their White counterparts, and their specific risk patterns and needs for AIDS prevention were unclear. Also unclear was the extent of diversity among Latino MSM in terms of sexual identity, sexual practices, lifestyle patterns, drug use, and involvement with mainstream institutions. Some Latino MSM could be identified at established gay bars, but it was not evident whether bars were a good recruitment site for reaching the full target population.

Despite a commitment to developing a project that was sensitive to and appropriate for the target population, problems were encountered in implementing the project that stemmed from limitations in the Council's familiarity with intragroup diversity among Latino MSM and with the values and concerns emphasized in different sectors of this population. Activities and approaches that proved to be effective in recruiting or retaining some individuals were inappropriate and uncomfortable for others. Thus, although a transvestite outreach worker was able to recruit other transvestites, he was unable to recruit many nontransvestite MSM. His replacement, an acculturated middle-class Latino MSM, was not effective with individuals who were unemployed, high school dropouts, or from rural Puerto Rican backgrounds. Only as the project gained deeper familiarity with the diverse social and cultural worlds of Latino MSM through ongoing applied ethnography, was it possible to become fully effective in reaching and serving the target population with AIDS prevention services.

━●━●━●━

The issues raised in this example are not limited to the implementation of public health efforts. Beyond health programs, particular hidden populations may be of keen research interest in evaluations of the impact of social policies (e.g., welfare reform), examinations of so-called deviance behaviors (e.g., criminal offenders), and in social needs assessments (e.g., in establishing programs to address social problems).

In all of the types of research just noted, social scientists commonly target specific "populations." A **population** is the largest group (or other unit) of research interest. For example, researchers may study runaway youth (a hidden population of growing research interest) with the intention of understanding the health risks that they face (e.g., street violence, exposure to the elements, poor nutrition, disease, drug use) and use this information to design interventions that address their health needs effectively. One way to go about answering questions about the health risks of runaways would be to interview and conduct medical examinations of runaways who are staying in homeless shelters. Because they are connected with an institution, these youth would be easy to reach, and studies of them would be less costly than would those of youth who are still on the streets. However, it may be that only some types of runaways seek out shelters for youth; others may avoid them completely. Moreover, it may be the case that shelter-avoiders have different or more severe health problems than do those who seek shelter residence. In other words, it may be inappropriate to infer the features of an entire population from a study of only one part of the population. Consequently, it may be necessary to go beyond subgroups of a population that are easier to find and recruit. In short, it may be necessary to identify ways to conduct effective research with population segments that are concealed from view to some degree. As this example suggests, hidden populations present significant challenges to the conduct of useful research,

Definition:
A population is the largest group or other unit of research interest

challenges that have led to the development of special sampling, recruitment, and retention strategies, all of which are addressed in this chapter.

There are many different types of hidden populations; notable examples include illicit drug users, such as injection drug users and crack cocaine users, as well as skid row alcoholics; commercial sex workers; recent inmates; school dropouts; unwed pregnant teens; nongay-identified men who have sex with men; transgendered individuals; street youth; gang members; criminal offenders; runaways; abused children and women subjected to domestic violence; carriers of genetic abnormalities or asymptomatic sufferers of infectious diseases (e.g., STDs, TB); the undocumented (illegal aliens); members of stigmatized groups who are "passing" as members of the majority population; sexual abusers and pedophiles; and the homeless. These are all groups whose existence is known but about whom we do not know a great deal. Moreover, they are groups that may be important to learn about because they have significant rates of health, mental health, nutritional, social, or other needs.

Even within these hidden populations, there may be particularly invisible subgroups. Among drug users, for example, some women may be especially hard to find. As Gross and Brown (1993) note, "women are less visible in semipublic settings because of the widespread pattern of men copping [buying] drugs for use in private" (p. 447) with their partners. Similarly, Hunt, Hammet, Smith, Rhodes, and Pares-Avila (1993), in discussing AIDS risk, observe that

> there is . . . another perhaps even more hidden population at risk for HIV infection [than injection drug users]: their sex partners. Partners of those injection drug users who are not injection drug users themselves are often not connected with traditional sources of contact with drug users [e.g., drug treatment providers]; nor are they always part of the injection drug

> user world in which some information is shared about human immunodeficiency virus (HIV). They are the wives and lovers of injection drug users who may or may not be fully aware of their partner's intravenous drug use. (p. 465)

Indeed, artificial groups, such as sex partners of drug users or school dropouts may be especially hard to find because they are composed of "individuals who happen to share a particular kind of experience but not necessarily with each other" (Kane & Mason, 1992, p. 212). There are no natural settings in which sex partners gather, institutions that they visit, or public records that indicate their characteristics or distribution.

From a research perspective, hidden populations are methodologically the opposite of "captive populations," such as prison inmates, clinical and hospital patients, students, and employees. Hidden populations generally are "neither well defined nor available for enumeration" (Braunstein, 1993, p. 132). With captive populations, by contrast, the universe is relatively well known, group boundaries are identifiable, and institutional records exist on the individuals who are members of the group. Moreover, captive populations are, by comparison, easy to reach.

Cross Reference: See Books 1 and 6 for a discussion of legal and ethical requirements governing research on "vulnerable populations"

Midway between hidden and captive populations are what might be called specialized "patron or membership populations," such as customers at a bar, theatergoers, or members of a church or club. Like captive populations, these individuals generally are easily reached, in that by definition, they must congregate at a particular site to be members of the group; however, like hidden populations, there may not exist any records to define the features of group members a priori. Of course, some types of patron and member populations may be more hidden than others, such as customers at a "biker bar" (a bar patronized by members of motorcycle gangs), bettors at an illegal gambling site (e.g., clandestine dog- or cock-fighting arenas), or members of a secret society (e.g., the Ku Klux Klan) or street gang. As this discussion suggests, it is reasonable to think of target research populations in terms of a continuum:

- Those that are well-known and highly accessible
- Those that are semi-hidden
- Those that are hidden
- Those that are quite invisible and (intentionally or unintentionally) resist research initiatives

Each of these types of target groups presents its own challenges to the development of good sampling designs.

Within each of the three hidden population types just listed, there may be considerable variability. In criminality studies, for example, it would be far easier to recruit a sample of petty street hustlers than it would a sample of "made men" (those who have undergone formal induction into the Mafia), even though both would be considered hidden populations. In either case, recruiting a *representative sample,* one that well reflects the range of characteristics of the wider target population, is very difficult.

As these examples reveal, the concept of hidden populations incorporates two somewhat different (yet intertwined) notions: On the one hand, it refers to populations that are *comparatively difficult to find and recruit* into a research project, and on the other hand, it designates *populations whose boundaries, characteristics, and distribution are not known.* Hidden populations often have both of these features. In some cases, however, the general characteristics of the group may be known, at least to some degree (e.g., because institutional records exist on the population), even though they are hard to find (e.g., school dropouts or runaway youth). In other cases, many members of the group are relatively easy to find, but their representativeness is unclear (e.g., the homeless) because the target population is dispersed and includes an unknown number of sub-groups with different coping and survival strategies.

Social concealment is a reflection of two social factors: *intentionality* and *capacity.* Some groups intentionally conceal their activities because they are illegal or otherwise subject to outside interference. Concealment in these cases is a consequence of active efforts to disguise or hide behavior. In their study of injection drug users, for example, Kane and Mason (1992) found that some individuals go to considerable lengths to camouflage their drug involvement in order to avoid arrest. They describe the case of Mike, a 42-year-old man who had been an injection drug user for 25 years at the time he was interviewed:

Definition: Social concealment refers to the distinctive feature of hidden populations, the fact that their behaviors and even their presence are hidden from public view and awareness

━•━•━ **EXAMPLE 3.2**

HIDING DRUG INVOLVEMENT

Mike says he has always wanted to avoid looking like a *dope fiend.* That means he tries to be clean and well shaved, he dresses nicely, and he is careful to avoid scarring his body with tracks [darkened scar lines produced by collapsed veins]. His maneuvering around the stigmatized image of the addict is an important survival strategy, for, as elsewhere, image counts for a lot in the streets. It has taken on an even greater significance in his efforts to avoid arrest as he gets older. (Kane & Mason, 1992, p. 205)

━•━•━

Stigmatization is another factor that propels concealment. Groups that are subject to social condemnation (on moral, religious, or other grounds) or even vigilante-style aggression commonly seek to hide their identities and activities. One such group is composed of transgendered individuals.

EXAMPLE 3.3   ━●━●━●━

STIGMATIZATION PROMOTES HIDING IDENTITIES

A cultural category or niche . . . among gay and bisexual men [and women] is . . . represented by transgendered individuals—those who are either transvestites or pre- or postoperative transsexuals. Transgendered males typically dress like females or at least androgynously. . . . Transgendered persons represent a particularly challenging population in that they are not well understood, experience considerable discrimination, and often have difficulty obtaining appropriate services. As with other marginalized populations, they tend to migrate to major metropolitan areas. . . . Although this subgroup is at extremely high risk . . ., there is a dearth of information available about their lifestyle. (Gorman, Morgan, & Lambert, 1995, p. 172)

━●━●━●━

Similarly, particular ethnic groups may be harder to reach than others because of the way they have been treated in the larger society, as Marín and Marín (1991) point out.

EXAMPLE 3.4   ━●━●━●━

STIGMATIZATION AS A RESULT OF ETHNIC DISCRIMINATION
PROMOTES HIDDEN IDENTITY

Hispanics could be expected to be more wary of researchers than are other ethnic or racial groups for a variety of reasons. Primary among these reasons is the concern that providing personal information may place some Hispanics at risk—for example, when income or immigration information could be used against an individual. In addition, some community members perceive social science research as a form of exploitation in which nonminority individuals reap the benefits of the data collection effort. . . . Concerns about participating in research are particularly salient when prospective participants are first contacted in person or over the phone. It is not uncommon for unscrupulous commercial firms to prey on the newly arrived and convince them to purchase unnecessary or expensive goods at high interest rates. (p. 42)

━●━●━●━

Other groups may be hidden but not as a result of intentional concealment. Like sex partners of drug users, these populations, though of special interest to particular research initiatives, may not recognize their "membership" in a particular population or be readily available for identification by researchers. Finally, there are populations that are hidden simply because they have not been identified as being of interest to researchers. Sex partners of drug users, for example, became of interest only because of the AIDS epidemic and the recognition that HIV could be transmitted both through sharing injection equipment and through sexual contact. Consequently, for a number of years, years during which HIV was being sexually transmitted to women, AIDS researchers and public health officials in the Western world conceptualized the disease as an affliction of gay men and failed to recognize and define similar and related symptoms among women as AIDS. In this sense, although reachable, women were a hidden population in the epidemic.

Second, there is the issue of *capacity.* Some groups have greater power to conceal their behavior than do others. Drug addicts, for example, include a wide range of individuals, from so-called street drug users—individuals who hang out on city street corners and "cop" (buy, borrow, or beg) drugs from street dealers—to physicians who practice in major hospitals and secure drugs through their own prescriptions. As this statement suggests, hidden populations are especially common at both ends of the socioeconomic pyramid. The rich, and especially the "super rich" (the wealthiest 1% of the population), generally are quite hidden because they have the power and resources to conceal their lives and behaviors from social science researchers. Consequently, far more is known about the lives of hidden populations among the poor than among the well-to-do (Domhoff, 1970). Even behaviors that have important effects on the lives of those who are not wealthy are hidden from view and general awareness. For example, wealthy philanthropists who choose anonymity often are able to achieve it despite the public impact of their contributions. Similarly, the wealthy frequently are able to hide embarrassing or even criminal behavior from public awareness. As a result, many social problems (e.g., child abuse, domestic violence, illicit drug abuse, alcoholism, teen pregnancy) popularly are conceived as characteristics of the poor and working classes rather than as being widely distributed across all social strata.

Strategies for studying the upper class—often from a distance (e.g., examinations of social registries from particular cities, enrollment in exclusive private schools, membership in wealthy businessmen's clubs, activities of exclusive resorts, and reviews of published marriage notices) —have been developed but are employed infrequently by social scientists. Generally, these strategies involve analyzing lists or other public or semipublic notifications used by the wealthy both to communicate their place among the elite and to enhance opportunities for interaction (and their children's interaction) with other "worthy" individuals.

Key point *This chapter will focus on approaches for studying disadvantaged and disenfranchised hidden populations because these are groups that are in need and at risk that may benefit significantly from improved applied social science research.* Overcoming limitations in our existing knowledge about these groups by examining their special features and thereby avoiding misplaced generalizations about them is the first objective of this chapter. The second objective is to call attention to the significant role of hidden groups in a wide range of contemporary health and social problems, thereby underscoring the importance of refining our techniques for studying these populations.

EVOLUTION OF HIDDEN
POPULATION RESEARCH

It is only in recent years that the study of hidden populations has emerged as a distinct field of social science research. Examinations of groups that fall within this domain of research, however, are not new. Although it is difficult to determine the earliest study of hidden populations, several candidate studies dating from the 19th century are noteworthy. In 1822, Thomas De Quincey published a book titled *Confessions of an English Opium-Eater*. De Quincey studied opium users at both the top and the bottom of the socioeconomic pyramid during an era when the use of the drug was not outlawed. Using a rough-hewn ethnographic approach, De Quincey sought to describe opium use among the working poor in London in the context of the impact of the oppressive social conditions in which poor people lived. In 1845, Frederick Engels published his book *The Condition of the Working Class in England,* in which he described the lives of members of the working class of Manchester. His account was the product of his extensive ethnographic wanderings through the unmaintained and filthy streets of Manchester's working-class residential districts.

Both of these studies stand out as very early efforts to acquire firsthand understanding of the day-to-day lives and experiences of populations that were socially discounted and largely unknown (because their lives were not granted much importance among policymakers and scholars of the day). The researchers in question were not completely systematic in their approaches to data collection, and their methods would be subject to some degree of criticism in the contemporary social sciences. Nevertheless, their findings about hidden populations were powerful, insightful, and historically significant. Beginning in the 1930s, there was increasing interest in the study of hidden populations, especially by researchers affiliated with the Chicago School of social research. Bingham Dai's *Opium Addiction in Chicago* (1937) and Alfred Lindesmith's *Opium Addiction* (1947) are important studies from this period. Concern with hidden populations has expanded significantly since the 1960s, as have the number of social scientific studies of diverse populations that fall within this rubric.

Procedures for finding and sampling hidden populations have evolved rapidly since the early studies, especially in recent years. Researchers at a number of sites have contributed to this process. Those involved in drug use and AIDS risk studies have been especially active in seeking to overcome the challenges of effectively sampling elusive populations. Some researchers have selected readily available samples, such as people in drug treatment, but then added on additional individuals recruited through other means, such as advertising, as a way to broaden the sampling frame. In Portland, Oregon, researchers ensured variability in their sample of injection drug users by recruiting from multiple sources, including a corrections facility, county health clinics, private welfare organizations, and street outreach. In Baltimore, researchers added sexually transmitted disease clinics and emergency rooms to the list of potential recruitment sites that would add diversity to the sample construction process. Another approach has been to begin with convenience and snowball sampling techniques—participant recruitment strategies that involve sampling in nonrandom ways among individuals who are readily available from the target population—and moving out along their social networks to recruit additional and potentially more hidden participants. All of these efforts have produced increasingly improved sampling approaches that attempt to draw on an ever-broadening cross-section and to be more representative of the invariably heterogeneous target population.

Over time, as described below and in Table 3.1, these approaches have been combined and refined to establish increasingly widely used procedures for studying hidden populations, and variants of the new approaches have developed in a number of research sites. The sharing of information among researchers across sites—a process that has been facilitated through forums created by the National Institute on Drug Abuse (NIDA) and other federal public health institutions in the United States—has allowed a mixing and merging of potential strategies, like those described below, for learning about, gaining access to, and recruiting hidden populations into research. These models all share important features (e.g., use of outreach). Although these models were first developed in the study of drug users, they are highly relevant to the study of all hidden populations.

The Chicago Model

Developed by drug researchers at the University of Illinois at Chicago in the late 1970s, this early approach combined **epidemiological** survey techniques, **street ethnography** focused on congregation sites of the target population, and the use of secondary data from institutional sources (e.g., drug treatment admissions) to identify and target heroin use social networks. The goal of this approach was to develop an understanding of a heroin epidemic in the city. Later, the method was adapted for use in studying the AIDS epidemic among drug users. The Chicago model typifies the movement in hidden population studies toward mixed quantitative/qualitative methodological approaches, a feature that characterizes much of the work done in recent years with hidden populations. The orientation of this work is to combine as many sources and kinds of data as possible to gain both depth (a more detailed comprehension of the target population) and breadth (insight concerning the

Definition:
Epidemiology refers to the study of the distribution, frequency, and determinants of disease and injury in human populations

Definition:
Street ethnography is the study of inner-city urban populations based on the immersion of an observant researcher in the day-to-day lives of the target group

Cross Reference:
See Book 1, and Book 2, Chapters 4–8, and Book 5, for a discussion of how these approaches can be combined

range and distribution of target population characteristics) in research understanding.

The San Francisco Model

The MidCity Consortium to Combat AIDS was one of the first research-driven HIV prevention projects in the United States to target street drug injection populations. In 1985, recognizing that drug injectors form a dispersed hidden population, the Consortium united street ethnography, key informant interviewing, theoretical sampling techniques, and **chain referral sampling** to develop categories of drug injectors within specified and mapped sampling areas within the city of San Francisco. Participants were then recruited from identified sections of the city. This approach evolved into the *targeted sampling strategy,* discussed later, that has become central to the study of drug use populations during the AIDS epidemic. A strength of this approach, one borrowed from the inductive orientation of ethnography, is flexibility. The project was designed to be interactive, allowing for modifications in the sampling strategy as new data were collected. The ultimate objective was to improve researcher confidence in the generalizability of findings from participants in the study to the wider, more hidden sectors of the injection drug user population.

Definition: Chain referral sampling involves using existing study participants to refer other members of their group for participation in a study

The Dayton Model

Building on the efforts of the MidCity Consortium in San Francisco, in the early 1990s, researchers at Wright State University developed a sampling approach for studying hidden populations of drug users that combines various sources of data, especially ethnography, to estimate the density of the target group residing in zip-code-defined areas of Dayton, Ohio. Through this approach, researchers were able to generate and use proportional sampling quotas for high-, medium-, and low-density zones of the city (based on the estimated number of target group members in each zone). This approach allowed researchers to shape recruitment to reflect the estimated characteristics of the target population. This model advances the targeted sampling approach toward greater confidence in the outcome of studies in which, as is always the case with hidden populations, it is difficult to know the full range of features and their distribution in the target population.

The Philadelphia Model

In 1987, the Philadelphia Health Management Corporation developed an approach to studying hidden populations that emphasized rapport building with relevant gatekeepers in the community. Designed to recruit out-of-treatment drug users, the model emphasized developing working relations with local drug dealers and shooting gallery operators, as well as local residents and merchants. Contact also was made with the police department. These efforts helped project staff gain access to individuals and avoid opposition to this access that might not have been possible otherwise. This approach revealed the importance of building a solid community foundation for studying hidden populations in minority communities.

The Hartford Model

A somewhat similar approach to the study of hidden populations was developed by researchers in Hartford, Connecticut. It builds on the data triangulation features of the San Francisco model but adds a strong emphasis on enduring community-based efforts that unite research with direct service provision, advocacy, and the building of com-

TABLE 3.1 Models Developed for Identifying and Recruiting Hidden Populations

Model	Distinctive Features
Chicago	Early effort to mix qualitative and quantitative data sources to gain a broader understanding of noninstitutionalized target populations, including the ethnography of congregation sites of noninstitutionalized members of the target group.
San Francisco	Adopts the multimethod approach to develop a target sampling plan as an advance over convenience sampling.
Dayton	Intensifies the use of ethnography to allow the development of proportional sampling quotas for high-, medium-, and low-density areas for recruitment of the target population.
Philadelphia	Uses a targeted sampling plan approach that emphasizes rapport building with relevant gatekeepers in the community to aid participant recritment.
Hartford	Implements a targeted sampling plan based on ongoing community-based organization service delivery to the target population and coalition building among research and service organizations.

 Cross Reference: See Book 1, and Book 6, Chapter 2, for a more detailed explanation of the use of ethnography in collaborative research partnerships

munity research capacity (Singer, 1993). Uniting the efforts of a consortium of community-based organizations—including minority community organizations, drug treatment providers, and community-based researchers—the Hartford model emphasizes collaborative research methods, anthropological field techniques, and the inclusion of community service providers in research efforts. This approach enabled researchers to move rapidly into diverse urban zones and work effectively in ethnically diverse populations while protecting against antiresearch backlash that sometimes develops in communities in the wake of university-directed research (for a summary of these five models, see Table 3.1).

Through efforts like these, researchers have been able to refine methods for studying hidden populations. The specific features of current approaches in hidden population research are now described in more detail.

Reaching the Hard-to-Reach: Methods
for Studying Hidden Populations

> ### Marking the Territory: Defining
> ### Target Population Boundaries
>
> - Targeted sampling: Mixing qualitative and quantitative methods
> - Mapping preparation
> - Secondary data sources: Exposed features of hidden populations
> - Ethnography
> - Ethnographic mapping
> - Finalization of the targeted sampling design

A significant challenge for the study of hidden populations is the establishment of target group boundaries, including setting inclusion and exclusion criteria for determining group membership. Decisions of this sort are necessary in research even though boundaries between groups often are fuzzy, membership can be transitory and situational, and insider definitions of essential in-group characteristics may conflict. Researchers recognize (or should recognize) that human social life does not unfold in discrete packages with well-defined and clearly demarcated boundaries. Nevertheless, some standards must be used to guide the selection of study participants.

Populations, it should be stressed, are social constructs. A population's existence *as a distinct group* is not so much given in nature as it is constructed by researchers (although not arbitrarily and always for a specific research purpose). Consider, for example, the population called "injection drug users," a term that is widely used in the AIDS literature for labeling a hidden population of considerable public health interest. In fact, this term achieved generalized usage only with the advent of the AIDS epidemic. Prior to this time, individuals who consumed illicit drugs through hypodermic injection were referred to as intravenous drug users. Recognition that some individuals "skin pop" (inject drug under the surface of the skin rather than in a vein) led to a terminological shift and, more important, to a broadening of the boundaries of the population of interest. Moreover, the drugs that people inject vary considerably. For example, some individuals have been found to be alcohol injectors. This practice, though apparently limited, is legal, but if syringe transfer between individuals occurs, it may be no less risky in terms of HIV transmission than is illicit drug injection (unless the alcohol kills the virus). In addition, research has shown considerable variation in injection frequency among drug users. To what degree is it likely that individuals who "shoot up" (inject drugs) one or twice per month are living the same lifestyle as those who shoot up eight times per day? Does a single behavior, in other words—one that exists in considerable variation (across class, racial/ethnic, geographic, sexual identity, and gender lines)—create a distinct population? In many recent studies of injection drug users, in fact, researchers have had to specify the timing of the individual's most recent injection as a criterion for recruitment (e.g., injection sometime within the 30-day period prior to being interviewed). It is far from evident where to draw cultural boundaries around drug injectors when studying an inner-city population in which drug use of various kinds is extensive and changing, while lifestyles among drug users and non-users have much in common because of the impress of harsh social conditions. In addition, it is important to remember that the category *injection drug user* may have little correspondence with the active social identities of those who inject drugs.

Similar problems are encountered in bounding other populations as well. People who engage in commercial sex work, for example, also are hard to delineate. For the most part, "street walkers" (usually down-and-out individuals who solicit customers by standing or walking along busy streets) form the popular stereotype of commercial sex workers. Nevertheless, highly paid "call girls" and escorts (who may live in exclusive apartments, attend college, and dress in the latest fashions) are also part of the population of commercial sex workers. Similarly, although commercial sex workers commonly are thought of as females, there are many male sex workers too, primarily, but not solely, catering to men who have sex with men. In addition, although the label "prostitute" implies a longer term illicit career, many individuals engage in commercial sex work for very limited periods of time or to raise funds for specific purposes. In our studies with inner-city impoverished populations in Hartford, for example, we have interviewed mothers who occasionally engage in commercial sex with specific known individuals (i.e., men they know in the neighborhood) in order to obtain enough money to be able to feed their children until their next welfare payment arrives. Similarly, some individuals may be taken care of by a "sugar daddy" but would deny that their sexual relations with this provider constitute prostitution.

In sum, the fixing of group boundaries for the purposes of research is a necessary if difficult task. In light of the discussion above, considerable caution must be exercised in avoiding unduly wide or narrow boundaries. Rather, researchers must strive to draw boundaries that are grounded in knowledge of the target group. Unavoidably, this means that boundaries may need to shift as researchers become more aware of the target population. This is precisely what occurred during the development of the San Francisco targeted sampling model.

Targeted Sampling: Mixing Qualitative and Quantitative Methods

Targeted sampling emerged as a methodologically reasonable solution to the difficult problem of sampling hidden populations. Despite known limitations, many researchers who study hidden populations have adopted targeted sampling as a method for participant selection. The purpose of a targeted sampling plan is to allow researchers to systematically develop "controlled lists of specified populations within geographic districts" along with "detailed plans . . . to recruit adequate numbers of cases within each of the targets" (Watters & Biernacki, 1989, p. 430). Targeted sampling relies on multimethod research (Bluthenthal & Watters, 1995) and is noted for mixing qualitative methods (to identify hidden arenas of behavior and social life) and quantitative methods of data collection (to ensure the generalizability of results). Although targeted samples are not random, neither are they convenience samples. Rather, they are a middle ground for achieving a sample that reflects best available knowledge about the target group when truly random sampling is not possible and when a higher degree of research rigor is needed than can be conferred through convenience sampling.

Key components of targeted sampling will be described using experience gained in Hartford, Connecticut, in developing and using a targeted sampling plan for a study of AIDS risk prevention among injection drug and crack cocaine users through the NIDA Cooperative Agreement for AIDS Community-Based Outreach/Intervention Research. The steps in the development of a targeted sampling plan including the following:

- Preparation for the mapping of indicator data on the target population
- Identification of available secondary data sources on the target population
- Ethnographic clarification of target group characteristics, behaviors, and distribution
- Finalization of the sampling plan

Mapping Preparation

The first step in the development of a targeted sampling plan involves geographically bounding the research area and establishing zones for data mapping. In San Francisco, during the development of target sampling as a recruitment method, this entailed an identification of those neighborhoods with the highest concentration of injection drug users and drug-related activity. In Dayton, Ohio, researchers used zip code boundaries to examine the distribution of concentration densities of drug users (Carlson, Wang, Siegal, Falck, & Guo, 1994).

━●━●━ **EXAMPLE 3.5**

TARGETED MAPPING IN HARTFORD

In Hartford, our research team, a consortium of five organizations composed of the Hispanic Health Council, the Institute for Community Research, and three other service agencies, divided the city in terms of the existing configuration of identified, bounded, and named neighborhoods. There are 17 such neighborhoods in the city. The city government has developed readily available maps of these neighborhoods, with streets drawn in, that proved to be very helpful in conceptualizing a citywide sampling plan. We knew various things about many of the neighborhoods from previous research as well as from general familiarity with the city. We knew something of the history of the neighborhoods, for example, and some of the ethnic transitions that had occurred within them over time. In addition, we knew which were high- and low-density residence zones and which were business or undeveloped zones (e.g., two neighborhoods had negligible populations). Also, we knew, at least roughly, about the general ethnic composition and the relative income levels in the different neighborhoods. In completing this first phase of the development of a targeted sampling plan, we ruled out neighborhoods with limited residential populations as potential target areas. For other neighborhoods, we pooled existing data from various sources, as described below, to get a better understanding of the distribution and composition of the target population across neighborhoods.

━●━●━

Secondary Data Sources: Exposed
Features of Hidden Populations

To help in the sampling frame selection process, researchers have, in part, turned to available institutional data sources. In different locations, different kinds of secondary data may be available and accessible. Unfortunately, researchers often have learned the hard way that data that have been collected by a governmental, educational, or other institutions may not be easily accessible because of turf issues, bureaucratic barriers, lack of staffing, outdated record-keeping systems, or disorganization. Sorting through which data exist and which are accessible, researchers have attempted to use multiple secondary data sets because of the inherent biases of any individual set. For example, relying only on arrest data would skew sampling frame selection to parts of the city where the police are most active or most successful in arresting members of the target population. Similarly, relying only on treatment or social service admission data could skew selection to those sections of the target area that have more treatment or service programs or more resources that assist people to get into interventions.

In studies of drug users, for example, a broad range of secondary indicator data sources have been identified (Braunstein, 1993; Wiebel, 1990):

- Law enforcement data on the location of arrests, seizures, and laboratory analyses of controlled substances
- Urinalysis results of new arrestees by home residence (e.g., performed by the Drug Use Forecasting System of the National Institute on Justice)
- Substance abuse-related emergency room admissions, including data from the Drug Abuse Warning Network
- Medical examiner (coroner) reports on the residences of individuals who died of drug-related causes
- Residence data on individuals admitted to drug treatment programs

- Prescription tracking systems for psychoactive pharmaceuticals
- Surveillance reports on identified AIDS cases by residence
- Admissions data on individuals treated for STDs, TB, or related diseases that tend to be prevalent among drug users

These indicator data sources are most helpful if they are linked with locations (e.g., residence) so that the information can be mapped (the location of each case identified and marked on a map of the targeted area) to assist in the location of high- and low-density areas (based on the frequencies of mapped behaviors or cases) for the target population. All of these sources of data are subject to some types of bias. The use of multiple sources collected by diverse organizations for differing purposes helps to limit systematic bias.

EXAMPLE 3.6

USING MULTIPLE SOURCES TO LIMIT BIAS IN TARGETED SAMPLING

Although all of the data sources noted above were not available in Hartford, we did have access to a variety of secondary data sources. In addition, we had data from a prior study we had completed of injection drug users and their sex partners. Data sources we used were the following:

- Our existing research data on the residences of injection drug users and sex partners recruited through convenience street outreach
- Our existing data on the residences of HIV-positive injection drug users and sex partners
- City of Hartford data on the residences of sexually transmitted disease cases
- City of Hartford Police Department data on the location of drug arrests for 2 years
- City of Hartford Police Department data on the residences of individuals arrested for drug-related offenses
- Drug treatment admission data on the residences of opiate users
- Census data on the sociodemographic characteristics of city neighborhoods

Potential sources of bias in these data sets are noteworthy. For data from our prior research, sources of potential bias include over-/undersampling of particular neighborhoods based on outreach worker preference, misidentification of individuals as drug injectors (which was based solely on self-report), participant provision of false residences, and changes in residence since the period of data collection. Our HIV testing data may have been skewed by a lack of representativeness of the sample recruited for testing and differential self-selection for testing. Potential sources of bias in arrest data lie in police attitudes about potential violators that shape arrest patterns and in geographic variation in law enforcement (e.g., disproportionately targeting ethnic minority neighborhoods for drug surveillance). Potential sources of bias in drug and STD treatment data include geographic, ethnic, and gender differences in access to treatment. Despite all of these possible sources of bias, the data listed above were collected by different institutions and groups with differing agendas and missions, and, hence, by relying on multiple data sources, it is possible to restrict skewing in any particular direction. For example, whereas drug arrests may "oversample" minority drug users because of prejudicial arrest patterns, drug treatment enrollment has been found to "oversample" white drug users.

Data from all of the sources noted above were entered by neighborhood or street address into a geographic information system (GIS) desktop software package, to enable us to summarize risk profiles for each of the major identified neighborhoods of Hartford. Comparisons show that findings from our prior studies, police arrest records, and STD and drug treatment records tended to fit together, with some neighborhoods having notably higher rates across all indicators and others having comparatively lower rates across most or all measures. GIS profiles on each of the neighborhoods were added to ethnographic information to complete our starting image of the distribution of the target group across city neighborhoods.

Ethnography

The key features of ethnography for understanding hidden populations are the following:

Cross Reference: See Book 1, Chapter 1, for a discussion of the critical features of ethnography

■ Its capacity for discovery of unknown social beliefs and behaviors

■ Its emphasis on "experience-near," on-the-ground research (Geertz, 1984)

■ Its emphasis on a holistic approach

First, although there is considerable opportunity for new discovery in most social science research, some research approaches are more open to encountering the unexpected than are others. Ethnography, as a form of naturalistic inquiry, is a highly porous approach that imposes little in the way of researcher control over the field of study; hence, it is quite open to serendipity, including the unearthing of patterns or relationships that are outside the awareness of, and thus are not self-reported by, research subjects. Ethnographers commonly enter the field with a set of issues of primary concern. Experiences in the field, however, have been known to send ethnographers home having carried out studies very different but locally more salient than the ones that sparked the research efforts in the first place. This emergent feature of ethnographic research makes it an especially important tool in the study of elusive populations and their potentially well-concealed behaviors. Second, as a context-sensitive approach, ethnography takes the researcher out of the academic or institute suite and into the street (or other settings) where members of the target population live out their lives. Through rapport building, concern with the subject's point of view, and long-term presence in the field, ethnographers often are able to gain access to places, events, and information that might be hard for other methodologists to achieve. Using level of participation in the lives of the target group as a criterion, ethnographic strategies can be said to form a continuum, with unobtrusive measurement lying at the least involved end of the continuum, participant observation techniques forming a middle ground, and intrusive strategies—those that take the researcher deeply into the lives and activities of the target group—forming the other end of the continuum. The relevance of each of these approaches for the study of hidden populations is examined below. Finally, ethnographers are able to use this access to move about, visiting and mapping the social scenes of target group life and thereby ensuring a holistic understanding of diverse and often dispersed group features, behaviors, and subgroups. All of these traits, which find expression through the data collection strategies discussed below, make ethnography an appealing approach in the study of hidden populations.

Key Informant Interviewing

Cross Reference: See Book 2, Chapters 4 and 6, for a broader discussion of in-depth and key informant interviewing

Ethnographers use the term *key informant interviewing* to refer to ongoing conversations with knowledgeable insiders (individuals from the target group) who are able and willing to work with them to produce an accurate, insider-guided picture of the target population. Although immersed in the target group—its lifestyle, culture, and social settings—key informants are individuals who are capable of stepping back from their involvement to offer objective accounts of group behavior, beliefs, experiences, and related matters. Good key informants not only answer ethnographers' questions, but to varying degrees, they also anticipate them. In other words, they grasp the ethnographer's objective, what he or she is trying to obtain (a full account of group life), and provide or help to acquire the needed information.

As the following two examples suggest, key informants are sources of two items that are critical to the successful study of hidden populations: information and access. Information provided by key informants can be used to evaluate the meaning of social indicator data, assess the validity and biases of such data, and check preliminary understandings that have been gained by reviewing institutional sources of information. By providing access to the target population, key informants help the ethnographer to determine the existence of as yet unidentified layers of target population members that should be represented in the study sample (Whyte, 1955).

━●━●━●━   **EXAMPLE 3.7**

THE ROLE OF KEY INFORMANTS IN PROVIDING ACCESS TO HIDDEN POPULATIONS

In *Street Corner Society,* a classic study of a hidden population (impoverished, inner-city Italian immigrants and their children), William F. Whyte described the important role that Doc, a street gang leader, played in his research. Whyte was an outsider; he did not know his way around, he did not know the local customs, and he was suspect to those inside the gang and the local Italian community. Doc taught Whyte how to avoid problems in the field (e.g., by not asking questions of people before his presence was fully accepted), and he took him places and introduced him to people. He taught Whyte that by being patient and unassertive in his research, in time, the information he needed would come to him. As a result, Whyte gained rapport with many members of the community and was able to develop a seminal account of a population that was otherwise resistant to examination by outsiders.

━●━●━●━

EXAMPLE 3.8 ━●━●●━

THE ROLE OF KEY INFORMANTS IN IDENTIFYING POLYGAMISTS
ENGAGED IN BANNED MARITAL PRACTICES IN UTAH

In my own study of polygamists in Utah—individuals who had been excommuni-
cated because they continue to practice banned marital customs of the early Mormon
church—research would have been impossible without the help of a key informant.
Because of laws against bigamy and opprobrium from mainstream members of the
Mormon church, Fundamentalists (as they call themselves) often lead quite secretive
lives. Historically, police raids have not been uncommon; hence, fear of undercover
agents is widespread. Through the friends and contacts of my initial key informant
(an individual who sought me out when he heard about my desire to study the
Fundamentalists), I was able to attend group meetings, interview many group members (male and female), and gain insight into life as an underground polygamist. This
work led to an ever-growing awareness of previously unknown segments of the target
group, including individuals who were still participating in the Mormon church
because their involvement in polygamy was so well hidden.

━●━●●━

Participant Observation

This is the core research strategy of ethnography, and it
is vital to the development of a targeted sampling plan. It
entails spending a considerable amount of time with research subjects in their natural settings as they perform
day-to-day activities, observing these behaviors and listening to the comments and conversations of subjects, and
recording this information as fieldnotes for later analysis.
In participant observation research, ethnographers approach members of hidden populations from a "one-down"
position. This means that ethnographers recognize that
insiders are the experts on their group. It is the ethnographer's responsibility to gain the trust and cooperation of
target group members rather than the other way around.
Accepting and validating the knowledge and experience of
the target population within their realm of specialization
(e.g., among the homeless, in finding shelter and food on

the street) is a means of laying the groundwork for the development of rapport. However, being "one-down" can contribute to feelings of uncertainty and caution on the ethnographer's part. Knowing that scheming or conning are common practices of economic survival among hidden populations, ethnographers attempt to approach their work with alertness, recognizing that study populations themselves appreciate the value of "street smart" behavior.

The objectives of participant observation in targeted sampling are described in the following example by Clatts, Davis, and Atillasoy (1995) and are based on a sampling design for the study of homeless youth in New York.

EXAMPLE 3.9

THE USE OF PARTICIPANT OBSERVATION IN IDENTIFYING STREET YOUTH IN NEW YORK

"One of the initial tasks given to the ethnographers was that of mapping the geography of the street youth population, that is, locations where youth were involved in prostitution, drug dealing, hanging out, eating, and sleeping. . . . A second goal was to identify differences within the street youth population that could be mapped by reference to time or location. . . . Ethnographers began research in areas where street youth were known to congregate . . . and moved into other areas as they learned more about the movement of the street youth population." (pp. 122-123)

This approach led to the realization that homeless youth are a diverse population, and that different kinds of street youth tend to congregate in different locations. For example, those found in the Port Authority Bus Terminal comprised the youngest group identified in the study; they were newer to street life, and they were more likely to engage in prostitution than drug dealing. These youth contrasted on all of these dimensions with those found hanging out in Times Square. This finding revealed the importance of including multiple sampling frames. Had the researchers assumed that the youth found at the bus terminal were typical of all street youth, they would have misunderstood the population, and they would have recruited from only one segment of a far more diverse group. Interestingly, in this case, life history interviews revealed that youth found hanging out at the bus terminal were not a distinct group but, rather, represented an early phase in the adolescent "street career." Learning about the lives of youth in Times Square in detail, for example, revealed that they, too, had previously hung out at the bus terminal and engaged in prostitution.

These findings are typical of the kind of discoveries made in ethnographic research. As this example affirms, social boundaries in the field are complex. Consequently, targeted sampling must, by necessity, remain flexible as new information about the target population is collected.

Unobtrusive Approaches

In addition to participant observation, ethnographers may employ various unobtrusive measures to assess density levels and behaviors for the target population (Webb, Campbell, Schwartz, & Sechrest, 1966).

EXAMPLE 3.10　　　➖•➖•➖

USING UNOBTRUSIVE MEASURES TO ASSESS BEHAVIOR OF HIDDEN POPULATIONS

In Hartford, we developed an assessment based on the discard of drug use paraphernalia, such as syringes, cookers (containers used to mix drugs with water), bottles of syringe rinse water, and crack pipes. Research team members systematically visited abandoned buildings, parks, alleyways, and open fields; using survey methods (walking through areas—eyes to the ground—to spot surface deposits of discarded drug use "works"), we identified places of drug user congregation and drug use (usually during times when no drug users were actually present). This information, including counts of identified items and descriptions of the site, were recorded. Syringes recovered at these sites were later tested for HIV antibodies to allow the mapping of infection patterns in the targeted areas. We also systematically visited pharmacies to interview pharmacists about the frequency of drug user purchases of over-the-counter syringes. Approaches like these allow ethnographers to add further information to their mapping of sampling areas without imposing on individuals who may wish to maintain their seclusion. Researchers in other cities have used similar techniques to identify commercial sex locations based on the discard of condoms.

➖•➖•➖

Intrusive Approaches: Going Somewhat Native

Some ethnographers have used approaches that are quite intrusive in the lives of the target population. At the intrusive end of the continuum, to gain participatory access to the target population, researchers may use techniques characterized by a degree of subterfuge. The classic and still controversial example is Laud Humphreys's (1970) study, published under the title *Tearoom Trade*, of a hidden population of men who have sex with men in public bathrooms. As part of his research on this population, Humphreys hung out in a public bathroom that was a frequent site for sexual encounters among men. He gained a role at the site as a lookout, warning men if someone was coming. However, he also recorded the license plate numbers of the men who participated in sexual liaisons in the bathroom, acquired their home addresses from the Department of Motor Vehicles, and visited their homes posing as a researcher conducting a door-to-door community survey of various kinds of behavior, including sexual practices.

A method that incorporated an even greater level of participation and artifice was developed by Ralph Bolton in his study of sex practices among gay men in Belgium.

Definition: Going native refers to situations in which ethnographers give up any semblance of scientific objectivity and become thoroughly enmeshed in the life and culture of the target group

Cross Reference: Book 6 includes further discussion of issues involved in the use of "undercover" research strategies

━●━●━ **EXAMPLE 3.11**

USING OBTRUSIVE MEASURES TO IDENTIFY SPECIFIC BEHAVIORS IN HIDDEN POPULATIONS: SELF-IDENTIFICATION AS A MEMBER OF THE GROUP

I spent most of my time, at all hours of day and night . . . , in settings where gay men in Brussels hang out: bars, saunas, restaurants, parks, tearooms, streets, and private homes. . . . My presentation of self was simple and straightforward: I was a gay man doing research as a medical anthropologist on AIDS and sex. . . . In my casual sexual encounters with men I picked up in gay cruising situations, my approach during sex was to allow my partner to take the lead in determining which sexual practices to engage in. Low-risk activities posed no problem, of course, but to discover which moderate and high-risk behaviors they practiced, I assented to the former (oral sex, for example) while declining the latter (unprotected sexual intercourse). (Bolton, 1992, pp. 133-135)

━●━●━

Through this strategy, Bolton was able to determine that high-risk sexual behavior was quite common and quite accepted in the privacy of the bedroom among gay men in Brussels. This finding was of importance because health officials in Belgium had come to the conclusion, based on several surveys, that gay men had significantly curtailed risky sexual behavior, and therefore, it was no longer necessary to focus prevention efforts on the gay community. However, because he did not formally tell his sex partners that *their* behavior was being studied until they advanced to unprotected sex, Bolton's approach, like Humphreys's, has been subject to criticism by some research ethicists.

Another approach for going beyond self-reported sexual practices in the study of a hidden population was developed by Terri Leonard in her research on male clients of street sex workers in Camden, New Jersey. Leonard conducted her research by hanging out at an inner-city "stroll" area (a street where sex workers seek business among the drivers of passing cars).

EXAMPLE 3.12   ➡•➡•➡

USING OBTRUSIVE MEASURES TO IDENTIFY BEHAVIORS IN HIDDEN POPULATIONS:
SELF-IDENTIFICATION AS A MEMBER OF THE GROUP

All men who attempted to solicit my services, assuming I was a sex worker, were invited to participate in a "sex survey." Men initiated contact using several approaches. Some pulled up alongside the curb or onto a side street and, with engines idling, engaged me in conversation. Some men parked alongside the street and got out to make a phone call or have a drink in a nearby bar, initiating conversation en route. Some men "cruised" by several times per day, several days per week, or once every few weeks before approaching. (Leonard, 1990, p. 43)

Leonard found that 20 men out of the 49 she was able to interview reported that they used condoms during commercial sex. However, despite this self-report, only five of the men actually had condoms with them at the time they solicited sex with Leonard. Like Bolton's work, Leonard's shows that more intrusive ethnographic approaches can produce data on hidden target populations that reflect actual rather than idealized behaviors.

Ethnographic Mapping

One of the common start-up tasks of ethnography is to draw a map of the geographic disbursement of the target group, their activities, and specialized activity areas. In part, this is done to help the ethnographer learn his or her way around, but it is also a strategy for ensuring the completeness, to the degree possible, of the researcher's gaze. Mapmaking allows ethnographers to systematically visit and holistically gather information about all spheres of target group life. In the study of hidden populations, this approach is adapted for use in sampling frame construction. As Bluthenthal and Watters (1995) indicate, the goals of ethnographic mapping in this kind of research are the following:

Cross Reference: See Book 2, Chapters 5 and 6, for a broader discussion of ethnographic mapping

- Gather information to compare and rank candidate zones or sections of the larger research area for possible selection as research sampling areas (in which to recruit study participants)
- Refine district boundaries
- Clarify in which zones contacts and key informants exist and where they must be cultivated
- Help establish sampling quotas for study participants located in identified zones

In the development of the targeted sampling plan for the study of drug injectors in Dayton, for example, ethnographers mapped the presence of six different types of sites in all of the 32 zip code areas of the city: crack houses, crack copping areas, drug shooting galleries (places where drug injectors pay for the right to come in and inject drugs), dope houses (places where drug injectors buy drugs and possibly inject them), injection drug copping areas, and drug injector residences (dwellings where injection drug users gather to inject drugs). Later, this information was used to calculate the relative density of drug sites in the zip code areas. A similar strategy was used in Hartford, with a focus on the mapping of all crack houses and shooting galleries/drug injector residences. This information was then compared to the rates found for the various social indicators to establish a continuum of drug use density across geographic units.

Finalization of the Target Sampling Design

In the final step, data from various sources, such as those just described, are triangulated to establish project sampling units, including, as in the case of Dayton, setting proportional sampling quotas (specific percentages of individuals to be recruited from each sampling unit based on the relative density of target population members present). **Key point** *By combining diverse data sets, developing them as indicators of target population density, comparing outcomes across the range of indicators used, and verifying suggested overall distribution patterns and distribution by subgroup types based on ethnography, researchers can be reasonably sure that they will be able to construct a sampling design that, unlike opportunistic selection, is reflective of the hidden population of interest.* In one sense, of course, targeted sampling plans can never be finalized, in that each research project produces new insights that lead to revisions in researcher conceptualization of the target group, its behaviors, and its distribution across the landscape.

This recognition has led to efforts to maintain ongoing monitoring of emergent behavioral trends and patterns in hidden populations of high interest. In this approach, research is not episodic (i.e., it is not organized into 3- to 4-year grant-defined discrete projects); it is continuous. The objective is to rapidly identify and monitor changes in the target population, as well as attempt to understand the forces driving the changes. Ongoing monitoring has the advantage of allowing very rapid recognition of new developments in the target population (recognition that may occur in advance even of many members of the target group who are not yet caught up in the new developments). Ongoing monitoring can be conducted through the deployment of field-based ethnographers, the use of mobile vans, or the establishment of field stations.

RECRUITING STUDY PARTICIPANTS

A range of methods, described below, is available for the recruitment of participants from hidden populations into applied research projects. Although these approaches are effective, researchers have accepted the fact that recruitment of many types of hidden populations requires the use of monetary or other incentives (e.g., facilitated access into treatment). In studies of out-of-treatment drug users, for example, the use of incentives is a standard practice. Methodologies that have been developed for recruiting hidden populations are street outreach, network recruitment strategies, mobile van approaches, and field stations.

Street Outreach Methods

Beginning in the 1960s, the practice of community outreach and the use of indigenous outreach workers became increasingly common in public health with the advent of the community mental health movement and other community-based health promotion efforts. Outreach is seen as a bridge that spans the social distance separating service providers and those in need of service, including hard-to-reach populations. It is intended as a mechanism that allows access to arenas of human life that are normally beyond the influence of mainstream social institutions. When tied to a targeted sampling plan, outreach becomes a tool for the selective recruitment of participants from designated zones and by specific subgroups (e.g., specified numbers of females). Outreach occurs "on the street, in public places, or in storefronts at the point of initial contact with the potential client for intervention services" (Hunt et al., 1993, p. 466). There are three criteria for evaluating outreach:

- Does it reach the target population?
- Does it successfully recruit appropriate study participants?
- Can it recruit participants again for follow-up assessment?

Definition: Indigenous outreach workers are those who come from and share characteristics of the target population

There has been much discussion in recent years about the use of **indigenous outreach workers**. For example, some have raised questions about the ethical implications of the common practice of sending former drug users back into drug use settings to recruit study participants. Risk of relapse is always great for individuals who are in recovery from an addiction; consequently, common practice in treatment is to help people avoid temptation by teaching and assisting them to avoid social settings and groups in which drug use occurs. Because of our concerns about this issue, some outreach programs targeted to drug users do not make prior drug use a criterion for the hiring of outreach workers.

The methods used by street outreach workers to find and recruit participants are illustrated in the following example, which draws from our work in Hartford.

USING STREET OUTREACH TO FIND AND RECRUIT PARTICIPANTS

Stowe Village is a large, low-income housing project on the north side of Hartford, Connecticut. During the summer of 1989, two outreach workers from our research team, Lucy and Angel, began visiting Stowe together as part of their daily effort to identify and recruit drug injectors for participation in a research project. On their first outreach visit to Stowe, these outreach workers encountered a group of young men hanging out on a street corner. They parked their car nearby and walked to the group. Several thoughts raced through the minds of the two outreach workers. On one hand, they attempted to spot visual clues that might suggest the men were injection drug users. They observed the men, searching for signs of nervousness and intranquility, which were indicators that they might be getting anxious for a "fix." On the other hand, they attempted to calculate the potential risk of walking up to the men. Would they be offended by the outreach workers' approach? Would they see the outreach workers as an exploitable source of cash or valuables convertible into cash? Would Lucy be subject, as she occasionally was while doing her job, to verbal abuse or sexual harassment? As they got close to the group, the outreach workers greeted the men in Spanish and told them they were HIV outreach workers. Reaching into their shoulder bags, the outreach workers pulled out the safety kits containing 1-ounce bottles of bleach, several condoms, and AIDS prevention literature being distributed by the project.

Lucy told the men, "I have some bleach and condoms in case you are interested." One man responded, "What do we want bleach for? We ain't got anything to use it with." When Lucy told the men they could always use it to wash their clothes, they laughed, and the first step toward establishing rapport was established. The outreach workers launched into an explanation of the project, including mentioning that it offered HIV testing and counseling, referral for health care social services, and AIDS education and counseling. In addition, they were told that they could earn $24 for participating in a 1-hour interview. One of the men, noticeable because he looked so tired and desperate, expressed interest. After further explanation, one of the outreach workers issued him an appointment card indicating a date and time that he could go to the project's Intake and Assessment Center for enrollment in the project. Because he lacked transportation and did not appear to know the location of the Assessment Center, the outreach workers provided him with a bus token and directions.

➤•➤•➤

As this account indicates, outreach, by necessity, requires that the worker *enter the target population's home turf—* places such as street corners, housing projects, shelters, and surplus food distribution sites of inner-city neighborhoods. The outreach worker *enters this field with an understanding of target population behavior,* an understanding born either from previous personal involvement in the group of interest or from being raised in the same community in which the target population is found. This knowledge is supplemented through *training* and prior outreach or similar *experience.* Training is geared toward developing a realistic understanding of the difficulties of working with hidden populations as well as an emphasis on treating program participants with respect, as individuals who have generously volunteered to assist the project achieve its goals. Furthermore, training must prepare the outreach workers to be sensitive to ethical issues in studying hidden populations, which will be discussed later. As Ronald Valdiserri (1989) notes in his book *Preventing AIDS,* the outreach worker who is an indigenous community member provides a *positive role model* and *credible information source.* Such a person may be more effective than other health workers in persuading at-risk individuals to participate in prevention research programs. The role modeling exhibited by outreach workers is expressed in their willingness to risk both potential arrest and bodily harm by inserting themselves into social settings in which danger is commonplace. Simply put, community outreach workers put themselves at risk daily to help others avoid risk.

Effective outreach hinges on *personal involvement with members of the target population.* Outreach workers get to know project participants, build rapport with them, and attempt to establish a trusting relationship based on genuine interest and concern. Developing good rapport with members of hidden populations can be particularly difficult, but studies show that demonstrating concern about a participant's well-being and providing useful and *nonjudgmental* information about how to get needed services are significant aids in the development and maintenance of good relations with study participants.

➤•➤•➤   **EXAMPLE 3.14**

DEVELOPING POSITIVE RELATIONSHIPS WITH HARD-TO-REACH PREGNANT TEENS

The Comadrona (the Spanish term referring to the traditional midwife) Program at the Hispanic Health Council in Hartford, Connecticut, includes a component that is specially targeted to pregnant teenagers. Pregnant teens often are unwed, and they may be living with a boyfriend or with their family of origin. Because of pregnancy denial, conflict with parents and/or boyfriends, and embarrassment, pregnant teens constitute an important hidden population. Commonly, pregnant teens are late to enter prenatal care, and the Comadrona Program was developed to facilitate this process and to provide case management that is designed to help educate the expectant mother about reproductive and maternal health, facilitate attendance at prenatal care appointments, and provide pre- and postpartum support and well-baby education. Clients enter the program through referral, walk-in, and outreach.

Outreach in the Comadrona Program includes several components, including going door to door to ask about pregnant teens in the neighborhood, following up on the pregnant friends of existing clients, and walking through targeted neighborhoods attempting to spot teen girls who appear to be pregnant. When pregnant teens are identified on the street, outreach workers initially engage them in friendly, nonjudgmental conversation, telling them "What a beautiful belly you have" and asking when they are expecting to deliver. When the outreach worker perceives that the girl is ready, she will ask if she is enrolled in a prenatal care program. If the girl provides a negative response, the outreach worker will then stress the importance of prenatal care and introduce the idea of enrollment in the Comadrona Program. As this account suggests, outreach workers attempt a seamless and natural progression that moves from a friendly conversation among women about women's issues into more directed client recruitment.

➤•➤•➤

Effective outreach requires maintaining a positive attitude toward both the work being done (public health research) and the people being reached. The starting point is *empathy*. Empathy begins with recognizing that other people's subjective reality may be different from one's own; their life experiences are different, their values are different, and the day-to-day world in which they live may be different. Empathy involves identifying emotionally with another person. It does not mean condoning all behavior; rather, it means understanding the behavior and the other person in the context of his or her life (i.e., to the degree that such a thing is possible, seeing the world through his or her eyes). A key part of the outreach worker's job is *active, sympathetic listening*. This means staying very conscious of what the other person has to say, staying attuned to both verbal and nonverbal communication, and taking the time to hear the speaker's core concerns. It may involve asking questions (e.g., "How did you feel about that") or expressing confirmatory remarks. Finally, it involves refraining from expressing judgments about the other person's behavior (while acknowledging to oneself the experience of negative reactions). In the end, good outreach means caring about the participants and respecting them as people. These approaches have proven to be effective in making hard-to-reach populations reachable and hidden populations findable.

Because outreach workers spend many hours on the street, often in inner-city neighborhoods with comparatively high crime rates, they must be on guard against sexual or other harassment or physical threats in the field. These concerns are handled to a large degree by remaining alert to risk and danger and through constant evaluation of risk during interactions with participants on the street. Training should emphasize that when outreach workers feel uncomfortable in a particular setting, they should leave as soon as possible.

Network Recruitment Strategies

Since the mid-1980s, a growing number of researchers have incorporated network concepts into the study of hidden populations. This work emerged from recognition that focus on the individual as the primary driving force in behavior is restrictive and fails to consider that most individuals do not live their lives independently of family members, friends, and acquaintances. Understanding people in their natural social contexts often requires an examination of social network structures and patterns that may channel behaviors of research interest. For example, the emergence of a new risk behavior in a drug-using population tends to spread along preexisting lines of social relationship. Understanding how these changes take place requires a shift in research focus and conceptualization from the individual to the social network level.

Cross Reference:
See Book 4, Chapter 1, for a more detailed discussion of social networks

Network approaches also constitute an alternative approach to participant recruitment. Consider the following example:

EXAMPLE 3.15

RECRUITING DRUG USERS THROUGH PERSONAL NETWORKS IN HARTFORD'S PUERTO RICAN COMMUNITY

In Hartford, we have begun to apply network approaches for studying the patterning of violence among drug users in the Puerto Rican community. In this joint Hispanic Health Council/Institute for Community Research study, we are using an ego-centered network approach. Outreach workers recruit out-of-treatment drug users who are interviewed about their past and present experience of and involvement in violence. These individuals are designated as Index Participants. As part of the interview process, these individuals identify members of their social networks, including members of their risk networks (those with whom they use drugs and have sex). Index Participants are then asked to recruit three members of their risk social networks to participate as Network Participants in the study. For each member of their network that Index Participants bring in, they are paid a small "finder's fee." If they are unable to recruit at least two network members, they are dropped as study participants.

As this example shows, in network studies, in addition to outreach workers, *members of the target population play a key role in the recruitment of study participants.* This approach opens access to individuals who may not have been successfully contacted or recruited by outreach workers (e.g., individuals who do not spend much time on the streets or in drug copping and use areas visited by outreach workers). Network approaches may be especially effective in reaching women, who are harder to reach than men through outreach.

In some hidden populations, of course, it may turn out that network approaches to research are especially difficult because of the fragile, shifting, and shallow nature of connections among individuals. At the same time, as the earlier discussion of sex partners of drug users suggested, there may not be network linkages among members of the target population. Still, methodologically, focus on networks is an important step in the study of hidden populations.

Mobile Van Approaches

Another approach for the recruitment of hidden populations into research is through the use of vans or other vehicles that travel to locations or neighborhoods that have been identified as likely target population contact sites. Vans or even recreational vehicles have been used in this way as temporary field stations in designated areas. These sites then become bases of operation for outreach workers and ethnographers who engage potential study participants in the vicinity of the vehicle. Individuals who meet study inclusion criteria and agree to participate can then undergo intake procedures in the van or sit down (perhaps over a cup of coffee) with an ethnographer for more in-depth interviewing. By regularly visiting the same sites over time, van-based outreach workers and ethnographers can begin to be known in various locations and develop rapport with individuals who live or congregate in the area. Use of the van allows outreach workers and ethnographers to have a safe haven and rest station in a new area of research penetration, limits the quantity of supplies (e.g., condoms, intervention and referral literature) that outreach workers and ethnographers need to carry with them, and facilitates the rapid intake of participants without requiring them to travel to a research center. Additionally, vans allow the easy transport and use of computers in the field.

A related approach involves the use of a service delivery van for recruitment and research. Several types of van-based health care delivery or public health promotion projects targeted to hidden populations are now in operation. Syringe exchange programs often are operated from vans that stop in or close to drug copping and use areas. Outreach workers and ethnographers ride with the van to its designated exchange sites and engage members of the target population at or in the vicinity of the parked van. This approach has been used in the evaluation of syringe exchange and also in other types of studies of drug-using populations. Primary health care and health screening vans that serve the needs of hard-to-reach clients or those in remote locations are another base of operations for researchers studying hidden populations.

Linking participant recruitment to mobile service or clinic vans entails certain limitations. Use of a needle exchange van as the sole source of recruitment for injection drug user participants, for example, limits the sample population to those who use such programs. Studies show, however, that many injection drug users do not make use of needle exchange (e.g., because they have alternative sources of sterile syringes). Similarly, limiting recruitment of the homeless to a mobile clinic would restrict participant selection to program users. As these examples suggest, multiple recruitment strategies expand the diversity of a study sample.

The Field Station

A related approach to the use of mobile vans is the fixed research field station. Field stations are research "outposts" located in the community of interest to the researchers. Like vans, field stations serve as bases of operation for outreach workers and ethnographers, but they can also house structured survey studies or even computer-based interview studies. Because they are located in fixed sites—often storefront spaces that are visible to the community—field stations can evolve into drop-in locations where members of the target population always know they can find a cup of coffee, snacks, prevention materials (e.g., condoms), referrals for service, or just other individuals for conversation. In other words, field stations have the potential to become established parts of local neighborhoods, and hence excellent places from which to conduct ongoing monitoring, as will be discussed later.

A significant variant of the field station approach is the development of research capacity in community-based organizations, as described earlier for the Hartford model. In this case, the field station can be a full or partial service center that immediately links research to the provision of services.

➤•➤•➤ **EXAMPLE 3.16**

BASING RESEARCH IN COMMUNITY-BASED SERVICE ORGANIZATIONS

The Hispanic Health Council is located in the center of the Puerto Rican community of Hartford. Shooting galleries situated in abandoned buildings, homeless shelters, drug copping areas, and a public park that is a regular site for drug purchase and use are all located in the area immediately surrounding the Council's Main Street building. The lobby of the Council is often filled with individuals who are awaiting appointments with their case managers, and they are sitting next to study participants awaiting appointments with interviewers. Ethnographers and outreach workers based at the Council have easy access to and a recognized base for work in the surrounding community. Nearby, across the street from a housing project that has long been the site of drug distribution and use, is the Institute for Community Research, a community research organization based in Hartford that collaborates with the Hispanic Health Council in the study of hidden populations.

➤•➤•➤

METHODOLOGICAL CONSIDERATIONS

Sampling Bias

Methodologically, the field of hidden population studies is driven by the issue of appropriate sampling. There are two issues here: knowing the population of interest well enough to construct a representative sample, and being able to recruit such a sample into the study. Sampling is a necessary feature of social science research because it would be impossible, due to limited research funds and lack of time, to study every member (i.e., what researchers call "the universe") of all but the most narrowly defined populations (e.g., members of a specific household). Because researchers are forced to sample from the larger population of interest, they are especially concerned that their research sample effectively *represents* the wider target population, allowing them to have confidence that inferences drawn about the sample apply to the whole population of interest. For example, if a researcher is studying pedophiles, and it is known that 10% of pedophiles are women, then the sample should reflect this proportion. Of course, the very reason the field of hidden population studies emerged was, in part, because it is concerned with groups like pedophiles whose number, distribution, characteristics, and behaviors are concealed; hence, it is difficult, a priori, to construct a representative sample. Failure to construct a representative sample can lead to biased results. Sampling bias is a major problem of all social science research, but it is of special significance in the study of unknown or poorly known groups.

Watters and Biernacki (1989) have identified a number of ways in which sampling bias can distort research findings. Their specific focus is on bias in sampling injection drug users, but their arguments have relevance for the study of all hidden populations. They note that although the largest portion of injection drug users in drug treatment are enrolled in methadone programs, the "bias introduced by sampling research subjects only in methadone treatment clinics . . . could lead to the erroneous conclusion that all injecting drug users are heroin addicts whose primary drug use involves daily heroin injection" (p. 417). A comparison of treatment-seeking and untreated opiate addicts, for example, found important differences in severity of addiction, risk-taking behavior, and level of social and psychological

 Key point functioning. *Basing interventions solely on the characteristics of those already in treatment could limit their appeal to and effectiveness with the wider population of concern.* The same point holds for all generalizations from institutionalized to noninstitutionalized populations. This issue is significant because of various studies indicating the necessity of matching patients to appropriate intervention modalities if treatment is to be effective.

Convenience samples that are drawn in whole or primarily from institutionalized populations may be inappropriate for generalization to noninstitutionalized populations because the behaviors of concern (e.g., behaviors that transmit diseases) tend to occur outside of clinical settings. Studies have shown that risk behaviors are significantly more frequent among noninstitutionalized populations than among those who are in treatment. At the same time, some behaviors of interest in hidden population research, such as domestic violence, may *only* occur outside of treatment settings.

The ethnic and gender composition of institutionally connected populations may be quite skewed relative to the population that is hidden from institutional intervention. In drug treatment, for example, women, and especially pregnant women, may be significantly underrepresented. Similarly, programs targeted to youth that are based on students may be inappropriate for and unappealing to school dropouts.

Behaviors of concern among hidden populations may be relatively rare in the general population. Attempts to understand injection drug use, for example, through general population surveys or even door-to-door community surveys reveal that this is an infrequent practice in the population as a whole. Gathering an adequate sample of drug injectors or pregnant teens through a general survey would be very costly. Therefore, understanding drug injection or many other behaviors of interest among hidden populations requires a targeted study designed to find and recruit individuals who engage in this behavior. This type of targeting tends to produce nonprobabilistic convenience samples. As will be discussed later, however, researchers who study hidden populations have developed methods for in-

Cross Reference:
See Book 1, Book 2, Chapter 9, and Book 3, Chapter 2, for discussions of sampling strategies

creasing confidence in the generalizability of their research findings.

Studies of hidden populations must confront four issues as they attempt to assemble representative, nonbiased samples: the precision with which a target group has been defined for purposes of research, the adequacy of the size of the sample, the internal diversity of the target group, and the level of concealment or embeddedness of the target group. By definition, it is difficult to precisely define hidden populations. Insufficient knowledge about the target group often encumbers definitional precision. Consequently, it is necessary to define geographic boundaries (e.g., members of the target group who live or are found within specified borders) and inclusion/exclusion criteria (i.e., specific traits, behaviors, or other qualifying or disqualifying features of group membership). As this implies, definitions of the target group are artificial (i.e., they are imposed by the researcher), but their use removes ambiguity about how the sample was constructed. Ethnography is such a useful tool in hidden population research precisely because it has the potential of limiting the artificiality of group definitions by grounding research parameters within the context of:

- actually observed behaviors
- insider understandings (e.g., cultural meanings, beliefs, values, expectations)
- self-reported identities of the target group; and the specific social scenes (i.e., locations, settings, socially defined occasions and events) that mark group activities

In this sense, the design of hidden population research is a carefully controlled balance between the research need to impose controls and the capacity of research techniques to avoid imposing false categories and boundaries on the target group (Kane & Mason, 1992). Targeted sampling, by imposing geographic or other boundaries for purposes of recruitment yet retaining the flexibility to adjust recruitment in light of newly learned information about the target group, reflects this tension between researcher control and social reality.

When the size of a target population is unknown, it is difficult to know the size of an adequate sample. For example, how many abused women would you have to interview to adequately represent the population of women subjected to domestic violence? Because it is believed that thousands of women each year are victims of domestic abuse (although the exposed features of this population are limited to actually reported cases), it is unlikely that interviews with five such women could very effectively capture the experience, social features, or health implications of spousal abuse. Researchers must grapple with the issue of sample size based on awareness of the target group and the need to perform statistical tests on associations between variables of concern.

The issue of sampling adequacy is directly linked to the degree of heterogeneity of the target population. A more diverse target group will, by necessity, require a larger sample if all of its diversity is to be effectively represented by the study sample. Researchers often use measures of statistical power to calculate sampling adequacy (i.e., procedures for measuring how large a sample is needed to test the strength of relationships that are found among research variables).

As we have seen, level of active concealment or passive embeddedness (i.e., like sex partners of drug users, lacking distinct group identity, congregation sites, or activities) is a major stumbling block in the construction of study samples of hidden populations. These factors make it difficult to construct random samples, because the size and dimensions of the pool from which participants would be randomly drawn is unclear. Consequently, hidden population studies limit sampling bias by using strategies designed to approximate structured random sampling (i.e., identifying population segments and selecting the sample proportionate to segment size).

Limiting Attrition in Longitudinal Studies

Just as they do for initial recruitment, hidden populations present significant challenges for retention in intervention or experimental studies as well as for follow-up data collection in longitudinal studies. Unfortunately, the impact of *attrition*—the term that is used to describe the loss of participants from a study—on intervention research is a significantly understudied topic. Many intervention studies with hidden populations fail to report attrition rates, and few analyze the impact of resultant selection bias on the validity of project findings. However, from a scientific perspective, the potential impact of attrition is severe—no less so than recruiting skewed samples that do not accurately reflect the target population—and hence, identifying strategies for limiting attrition in studies with hidden populations is of utmost importance.

There are many reasons why individuals may be lost to a research project. They may move away, become ill, be arrested, or even die. In studies with drug users, all of these factors contribute to both loss to intervention and loss to follow-up. Additionally, individuals may have bad experiences in research (e.g., they may feel that an interviewer was disrespectful or asked intrusive questions) that lead them to decide to end their participation. Also, they may find work, enter into a treatment program, begin school or a training program, or grow fearful that their confidentiality will be breached. With hidden populations, all of these potential reasons for attrition are multiplied because such populations often are attempting to avoid the police or other government institutions, keep their activities secret, handle numerous health risks, cope with the consequences of poverty and unstable housing, and avoid street violence.

Tracking techniques and incentives have been suggested as means of limiting attrition in hidden populations. Still, reducing attrition from data collection in studies of these populations remains a difficult task. Consequently, approaches have been suggested for using statistical techniques to compensate for missing data caused by participant attrition. However, questions have been raised as to whether such techniques are adequate to estimate the true effects of an intervention with a high loss of participants before follow-up. Without understanding the effect of attrition in a specific type of program, it is unlikely that appropriate adjustments can be implemented.

Consequently, special efforts are needed to retain participants in longitudinal studies of hidden populations. A review of effective methods to track these populations has been developed by Desmond, Maddux, Johnson, and Confer (1995). They identify 10 strategies:

(a) collecting complete locator information (e.g., in addition to common items such as address and phone number, information on a participant's social security number, relatives' addresses and phone numbers, common hang-out areas, and the location where the participant's mail is delivered) at the start of the intake interview

(b) fully informing participants about follow-up interview requirements

(c) providing adequate monetary incentives (participant fees)

(d) hiring ethnically and experientially appropriate staff

(e) documenting all follow-up work

(f) making exhaustive use of institutional information about participants (e.g., welfare files)

(g) streamlining the follow-up data collection to make the procedure as rapid as possible

(h) conducting follow-up interviews in a mutually acceptable location

(i) providing travel support for participants to the interview site

(j) building in adequate time for follow-up data collection with the entire project sample.

Additional strategies have been suggested by Cottler, Compton, Ben Abdallah, Horne, and Claverie (1996), including expanding locator data collection to include the maximum number of items possible; updating locator information at each subsequent follow-up interview; attaching incentives to intervention sessions; and implementing a three-stage tracking methodology that incorporates phone tracking (regular phone calls to participants), systems tracking (using available health, social service, or criminal justice computer tracking programs on the target population), and field tracking (home visits and street ethnography).

Other strategies that have been used by hidden population researchers include:

- employing street-aware outreach/interviewers
- picture taking of all participants at intake (for use in follow-up recruitment)
- conducting brief, paid, postintervention session evaluation interviews and offering an incentive bonus to individuals who complete all intervention sessions
- conducting brief contact interviews at periodic intervals to ensure regular interaction with participants during the follow-up period
- sending postcard reminders to participants; identifying and regularly visiting all congregation points
- maintaining positive relations with community agencies and other providers to allow participant tracking
- community newspaper checks to identify arrests of study participants
- fully informing participants about the benefits of applied research
- ensuring that project staff build sensitive, supportive, and trusting relations with participants
- using a wide variety of posters, radio announcements, and flyers to publicize follow-up interviewing
- maintaining contacts with researchers in other cities where participants may migrate.

In studies of drug users in Hartford—a city with high attrition rates due to particularly high rates of HIV infection among injection drug and crack cocaine users, comparatively high participant arrest rates, high frequencies of drug injection, and a notably mobile population—researchers have tested a number of additional approaches, including the following:

- House-to-house visits to "abandoned" apartment buildings (where numerous homeless people, in fact, reside in Hartford)
- Rapport building with the "house men" (owners or managers) at local drug shooting galleries and crack houses to allow drop-in visits for the purposes of participant contact
- Use of the inmate computer tracking system maintained by the state Department of Corrections
- Provision of AIDS education sessions to allow regular contact with homeless shelter residents
- Identification of homeless encampments hidden under densely wooded highway overpasses and along the Connecticut River
- Nighttime emergency room checks at the three local hospitals

Each of these strategies allowed the researchers to find missing participants for follow-up interviewing.

Follow-up with hidden populations remains a difficult assignment. Using relocation strategies such as those just noted have enabled the inclusion of these populations in successful longitudinal studies.

Reliability and Validity

In all studies, researchers must confront issues of *reliability* and *validity*. The former term addresses issues of consistency (e.g., Does a homeless individual report the same life history information each time he or she is interviewed?), whereas the latter is concerned with issues of accuracy (e.g., Does a research instrument designed to study risk behaviors of people with sexually transmitted diseases actually mea-

Cross Reference: See Book 1, Book 2, Chapter 10, and Book 3, Chapter 2, for discussions of reliability and validity in ethnographic research

sure the issue of concern?). Given the special problems of studying hidden populations; the health, residential, and other difficulties that individuals in such populations commonly face in their lives; and the dearth of baseline information available when studies of these populations are being designed, it is not surprising that reliability and validity are especially thorny problems in this arena of social science research. Consequently, it is particularly important to incorporate reliability and validity checks—research procedures for routinely examining the quality and dependability of the data being collected—in studies of hidden populations.

The reliability of data is established when measures taken by two different researchers or the same researcher at two or more points in time are the same. For example, researchers may wish to rate the level of health risk faced by homeless individuals (e.g., to assess whether those who stay at shelters experience greater or lesser risk than those who do not). During interviews, homeless individuals can be asked a series of questions about risk behavior and experiences. A set of judges (e.g., other researchers not involved in the study) can then be asked to establish, based on the number, kind, and frequency of risk, to rank an individual as being at high, medium, or minimal health risk. Having two or more judges independently rank the same individuals can be used as a check on **interrater reliability**. Alternately, some researchers have compared findings on face-to-face interviews with those from computer-driven interviews to test the reliability of research findings. In longitudinal studies in which members of hidden populations are interviewed two or more times over the course of a period of study, the data produced can be considered reliable if an individual's answers are consistent for items that are not expected (in most instances) to change over time (e.g., ethnicity, gender, place of birth, date of first use of drugs, etc.). Assessment of congruence on *stable features*

Definition: Interrater reliability refers to the degree of correspondence among researchers in ratings, rankings, or coding decisions

(traits that are constant over time for most individuals, such as gender) and *established features* (attributes that, once established, cannot be undone, such as "ever slept in a homeless shelter") can serve as a reliability check in longitudinal research.

As noted, validity refers to the accuracy of data. For example, in a study of access to drug treatment among out-of-treatment drug users, researchers must establish that study participants are, in fact, drug users (and not just individuals seeking to be paid for conducting an interview). Urine toxicology (a chemical check for the presence of substances in a urine sample) often is used to validate self-reported drug use.

There are various threats to the validity of a study (Campbell & Stanley, 1963). Some factors may jeopardize a study's *internal validity,* whereas others threaten *external validity.* The first of these refers to the validity of inference on the targeted study population. In addition to threats posed by errors in information collection or unrecognized baseline differences between comparison groups (e.g., in a study contrasting the efficacy of two alternative intervention models designed to lower risk in a target population), selection biases may distort estimates of the intervention effect in the targeted study group. If comparison groups (e.g., those assigned to the experimental group vs. those assigned to the intervention group) experience differential dropout rates in an intervention resulting in altered baseline risk in the experimental and comparison groups, measures of outcome differences may be invalid.

External validity refers to the degree to which outcomes are peculiar to the special conditions of the study or can be generalized to conditions beyond those of the study. For example, can the findings on a study of "bottle gang" behavior (i.e., collectively acquiring and sharing drinks from a common bottle) among skid row alcoholics in downtown Los Angeles be generalized to all skid row alcoholics in the country, only to skid row alcoholics in the West, only to those in Los Angeles, or only to those who actually participated in the study? Can the findings be generalized only to specific times of the year (i.e., because people may be forced to behave differently as the weather changes), only to big-city social settings, or only to members of specific ethnic groups? The answers to these questions lie in the representativeness of the sample population and the research setting to the population universe and the wider set of contexts in which the target population is found. Limitations on representativeness restrict the generalizability of findings. In the study of hidden populations, researchers are constantly struggling with the issue of representativeness and, hence, with the generalizability of their research results.

Experimental studies with hidden populations face important threats to validity because of the difficulty of retaining these populations in interventions or relocating them for follow-up. For example, attrition threatens external validity to the degree that subjects who remain in a study are systematically different from those who drop out. Existing attrition research shows that attrition can have consequential effects on intervention effectiveness. In a study of an adolescent smoking prevention program, the heaviest smokers were the most likely to drop out of the treatment group but not the control group. Dropouts generally were heavier alcohol and drug users, were more likely to associate with other smokers, and had lower educational goals than did program completers. Because of the greater loss before follow-up of heavy smokers in the treatment group, findings interpreted without factoring in the probable effect of selection bias would suggest that the intervention was more effective than was warranted. This finding is supported by research showing external validity problems that result from the tendency of the heaviest substance users to drop out of intervention.

Various other factors can weaken the external validity of a study. The recruitment interaction or instruments used to measure the target population at baseline may influence the reaction of study participants to an intervention. For example, outreach workers, when recruiting participants into a study, may inadvertently influence participant behavior (e.g., by sharing prevention information about risky behavior). Additionally, the setting of an intervention may threaten external validity. Will the findings of an intervention conducted in a hospital setting with homeless individuals be the same if the intervention is conducted in a homeless shelter? If the setting of the intervention influences the behaviors of concern, then generalizability to other conditions is not possible. Finally, because various interventions are targeted to hidden populations, involvement in prior intervention may affect outcomes on the intervention being tested. If participants from the target population have experienced a prior intervention in their locale, findings may not be generalizable to individuals in another city that did not implement the prior intervention. For example, an intensive public health mass media campaign on condom use previously implemented in the target city may make it difficult to generalize the findings of a condom skills-building intervention for commercial sex workers to other cities that lacked the public health campaign.

All of these threats to external validity must be considered in designing studies with hidden populations and with the reporting of research findings.

ETHICAL ISSUES

All research with human populations must confront a range of ethical issues. Since World War II (and in light of Nazi experimentation with human subjects), standards of ethical conduct in research have developed. These standards include the following:

- Respecting study participants as autonomous individuals (in part by ensuring that their involvement in research is completely voluntary and based on fully informed personal consent)

- Treating study participants with beneficence and avoiding maleficence (in part by limiting their exposure to risk)

- Seeking to be fair to study participants (in part by avoiding discrimination or a re-creation of historical patterns of social inequality in the distribution of all benefits and risks of research participation)

Cross Reference:
See Books 1 and 6 for details about institutional review boards and ethical treatment of study participants

In some cases, institutional review boards have concluded that particular hidden populations, such as homeless adolescents under the age of 16, are not yet able to provide fully informed personal consent to participate in a research project. Consequently, they have refused to give approval for the study of these populations, making them, in effect, not just hidden but unstudiable populations. In other cases, questions have been raised about the capacity of various groups (e.g., long-term skid row alcoholics) to give fully informed consent because of mental health impairments. For the most part, however, review boards have not blocked the study of hidden populations. Nevertheless, there are a number of special ethical issues that arise in the study of these populations that merit specific attention.

These issues stem from several sources, including the involvement of study participants in illegal or dangerous activities, the collection of highly sensitive information on participant activities, the recruitment of individuals with significant health and social service needs, and the potential exposure of project staff to risky settings. Given the serious (even life-and-death) nature of the ethical issues confronted in the study of hidden populations, careful review of ethical issues that may be confronted and thorough training in how to avoid or, if necessary, respond to ethical dilemmas is a critical component of project implementation.

Maintaining Confidentiality
With Highly Sensitive Data

Hidden populations often want to stay hidden or at least conceal certain behaviors, such as drug use or involvement in other illegal activities (drug dealing, prostitution, gambling, theft, physical violence, etc.). Moreover, some research on hidden populations (e.g., AIDS research) focuses on very private behaviors, such as sexual activity. As a result, studies of hidden populations often produce highly confidential information. Fully protecting the confidentiality of research participants (from the police, the courts, insurance companies, creditors, employers, other research participants, etc.) is a fundamental responsibility of researchers. In federally funded research, an array of procedures (e.g., subject consent to research protocols) must be followed to protect confidentiality. Universities and research institutes commonly have committees to review risks to human subjects in research projects and to ensure the enforcement of protections. Additionally, procedures have been established at the federal level to protect research records from seizure by the police.

Cross Reference: See Book 1 and Book 6, Chapter 1, for further discussion of confidentiality

In spite of these protections, there is always a potential risk that participant confidentiality might be breached. For example, drug researchers may inadvertently schedule simultaneous interviews with two individuals who are involved in a relationship but conceal their drug use from their partner, and they encounter each other unexpectedly at the research site. More commonly, confidentiality is breached because, over the course of a research project, adherence to human subject protocols slackens. Good training procedures for project staff, with regular updates and refresher courses, is critical. Keeping participants' names or other identifying materials (e.g., photographs, locator forms) separate from interview data (so that linkage by those outside the project would be difficult) is of equal importance. Consistent use of locked filing cabinets and password-controlled computer files is another important requirement of research with hidden populations. Most important, researchers must give careful thought to all potential avenues through which confidentiality might be violated and regularly monitor to ensure that protections are in place and are being followed.

Working With Populations at High Risk: Educational and Intervention Responsibilities

Another ethical issue confronted in the study of hidden populations concerns the responsibilities of the researcher relative to the health needs of research subjects. If researchers see study participants engaging in highly risky behavior (e.g., directly sharing syringes during drug injection), are they obligated to intervene in some way? Is it ethical to study such behavior and to record fieldnotes without offering intervention or prevention information? If a research participant is known to a research project to be HIV positive and then shares information about unprotected sexual behavior, what are the responsibilities of researchers to notify the individual's sex partner(s)? If participants share information about illegal activities, are researchers obligated to report this information to the police? If participants report their role in ongoing acts of physical or emotional violence, should researchers take some action to stop the behavior? These are just a few of the ethical questions that confront researchers studying hidden populations. Unfortunately, there is no uniformity of opinion about the appropriate response to many of these questions. Some university review boards have taken the position that researchers must report all illegal behavior described by participants to the police. This type of requirement would effectively terminate many studies of hidden

populations. Most ethicists, however, have sought to identify a middle ground that will allow research on hidden
populations to proceed while standards are put in place to
ensure that researchers do not shirk responsibility to intervene where appropriate and possible.

Studying Populations With Significant Health and Social Needs

A related ethical question concerns the responsibilities
of researchers to mobilize available resources to address the
often considerable economic, emotional, health, and human service needs of participants. If researchers encounter
pressing health or social problems in the populations they
study, are they responsible for having mechanisms in place
for intervention, or at least for referral? Should researchers
offer referral (called *active referral*), or should they make
referrals only if participants issue a request for assistance
(called *passive referral*)? These are important questions that
must be confronted when studying many hidden populations. Moreover, researchers who have worked with such
populations have found that these populations tend to have
complex, intertwined, and pressing needs, as well as complex entanglements with significant others, the courts,
landlords, drug dealers, and others that make it difficult to
know where to start and how best to intervene.

There are no simple approaches to this issue. Most researchers arrange at least passive referral linkages with
health care, mental health, drug treatment, and social service providers, whereas others offer more active assistance
in helping to ensure that participants are able to keep their
referral appointments and actually receive services. Which-
ever approach is adopted, it should be considered prior to
the initiation of research, and linkages and referral procedures with local providers should be in place prior to the
start of data collection. It is also important to consider the

stress placed on project staff who are involved in working with hidden populations. Constant exposure to suffering and feelings of inadequacy in responding to the problems faced by study participants can lead to staff burnout. Consequently, staff support and stress reduction mechanisms (e.g., staff debriefings, support groups, training sessions) may be needed, including, if available, the utilization of professional employee assistance programs.

Protecting Field Staff

In the study of hidden populations, researchers have a special responsibility to address the potential risks faced by project staff. These risks include exposure to theft, violence, and disease. Hidden populations among oppressed social classes have disproportionately high rates for all of these threats to emotional and physical well-being that can, in various ways, affect the lives of researchers. Discussing the use of field stations, Goldstein, Spunt, Miller, and Bellucci (1990) make the following comments.

EXAMPLE 3.17   ➤•➤•➤

DEALING WITH THEFT AND VIOLENCE IN THE FIELD

Theft and violence are two issues that must be dealt with when trying to operate an ethnographic field station. Tape recorders, jackets, cash, tools, coffeemakers, and a clock have been stolen from field sites. Thefts are typically difficult for staff members to accept and are often perceived as a violation of the trust between subjects and field researchers. Sometimes staff members interpret a theft as meaning that they have personally failed as researchers, that they are outsiders and "marks," and their feelings of being accepted by subjects were just illusions. Victimized staff members may need informal therapy lest feelings of resentment and suspicion color their interactions with subjects and render them less effective. (p. 90)

➤•➤•➤

Although not very common, incidents of violence or threats made to researchers also have been reported. Sometimes, violence has occurred as part of a theft, such as a mugging; at other times, it is the result of subjects blaming researchers for some misfortune (e.g., an arrest) that they have suffered. Occasionally, violence is not specifically directed at the researchers but a consequence of being at the wrong place at the wrong time. Preparation for handling these issues; staff training to minimize exposure to risk (e.g., arming field workers with cell phones, training staff to recognize their own role in theft by leaving valuable items exposed and to understand the street survival strategies of target populations); clear-cut protocols about appropriate and inappropriate behaviors in the field (e.g., not carrying money or other unnecessary valuables, leaving situations that seem threatening, establishing rapport and gaining approved access to sites where illegal activity occurs, building relationships among residents in target neighborhoods); and useful ways of handling threatening situations (e.g., conflict reduction strategies) generally are a prerequisite of field studies of hidden populations.

Exposure to disease is another potential risk faced by project staff. Airborne infectious diseases, such as tuberculosis, are especially problematic because they do not require staff to actually participate in overt risk behaviors. Similarly, easily spread diseases such as hepatitis must be considered as potential risks to staff. Other diseases that may be disproportionately common in some target populations, such as sexually transmitted diseases and AIDS, generally are not threats to staff unless they engage in specific risk behaviors, many of which may be violations of accepted ethical standards for the researcher/subject relationship. Training in risk avoidance (often available from the Red Cross, city health departments, or local community organizations); periodic testing for exposure; and clear-cut protocols for appropriate staff behavior are all important strategies for preventing the spread of infectious diseases among project staff.

CONCLUSIONS

The concept of the hidden population emerged in the social sciences as researchers concerned primarily with substance abuse and other public health issues confronted the fact that populations that were most accessible, such as those in treatment programs, prisons, and hospitals, were not necessarily a fair representation of the broader population of interest. Other segments of the target population were not "in" or connected to (or served by) health and social institutions. These individuals were significantly harder to reach and harder to enumerate. This meant that even if segments of the population of interest were reachable, it would still be difficult to ensure representativeness in research samples unless all segments and their relative distribution and frequency were known. At this point, researchers started referring to these populations as "hidden" and began to tackle the problem of how to study them. The methodologies that have been developed for gaining access to, sampling, and recruiting hidden populations have been described and illustrated in this chapter. This review affirms that it is possible to study various kinds of hidden populations but that researchers must give careful thought to the following:

- Sampling procedures and threats to reliability and validity
- Sources of secondary data that may be available
- The commitment of resources to the development of a locally grounded target sampling plan
- The recruitment and development of a trained cadre of indigenous outreach workers
- The selection of ethnographers able and willing to focus their research efforts on the target population of interest and the social settings in which they are found

- The resources needed for motivating target group participation in research
- The development of a common mission, language, and esprit de corps in a multidisciplinary team of ethnographers, outreach workers, and others
- The establishment of linkages with service providers for recruitment and referral for services
- The ethical dilemmas confronted in the study of elusive populations
- The patience needed to work with individuals whose lives often are seen (by outsiders and, to varying degrees, by insiders as well) as chaotic, self-destructive, and, at times, filled with suffering

These challenges are considerable but surmountable, especially in light of the significant potential contributions of good applied research with these populations.

REFERENCES

Bluthenthal, R., & Watters, J. (1995). Multimethod research from targeted sampling to HIV risk environments. In E. Lambert, R. Ashery, & R. Needle (Eds.), *Qualitative methods in drug abuse and HIV research* (NIDA Research Monograph 157, pp. 212-230). Rockville, MD: National Institute on Drug Abuse.

Bolton, R. (1992). Mapping terra incognita: Sex research for AIDS prevention—An urgent agenda for the 1990s. In G. Herdt & S. Lindenbaum (Eds.), *The time of AIDS* (pp. 124-158). Newbury Park, CA: Sage.

Braunstein, M. (1993). Sampling a hidden population: Noninstitutionalized drug users. *AIDS Education and Prevention, 5,* 131-139.

Campbell, D., & Stanley, J. (1963). *Experimental and quasi-experimental designs for research.* Boston: Houghton Mifflin.

Carlson, R., Wang, J., Siegal, H., Falck, R., & Guo, J. (1994). An ethnographic approach to targeted sampling: Problems and solutions in AIDS prevention research among injection drug and crack-cocaine users. *Human Organization, 53,* 279-286.

Clatts, M., Davis, W. R., & Atillasoy, A. (1995). Hitting a moving target: The use of ethnographic methods in the development of sampling strategies for the evaluation of AIDS outreach programs for homeless youth in New York City. In E. Lambert, R. Ashery, & R. Needle (Eds.), *Qualitative methods in drug abuse and HIV research* (NIDA Research Monograph 157, pp. 117-135). Rockville, MD: National Institute on Drug Abuse.

Cottler, L., Compton, W., Ben Abdallah, A., Horne, M., & Claverie, D. (1996). Achieving a 96.6 percent follow-up rate in a longitudinal study of drug abusers. *Drug and Alcohol Dependence, 41,* 209-217.

Dai, B. (1937). *Opium addiction in Chicago.* Shanghai: Commercial Press.

Desmond, D., Maddux, J., Johnson, T., & Confer, B. (1995). Obtaining follow-up interviews for treatment evaluation. *Journal of Substance Abuse Treatment, 12,* 95-102.

Domhoff, W. (1970). *The higher circles.* New York: Vintage.

Geertz, C. (1984). "From the native's point of view": On the nature of anthropological understanding. In R. Shweder & R. LeVine (Eds.), *Culture theory: Essays on mind, self and emotion* (pp. 123-136). Cambridge, UK: Cambridge University Press.

Goldstein, P., Spunt, B., Miller, T., & Bellucci, P. (1990). Ethnographic field stations. In E. Lambert (Ed.), *The collection and interpretation of data from hidden populations* (National Institute on Drug Abuse Research Monograph Series #98, pp. 80-95). Rockville, MD: National Institute on Drug Abuse.

Gorman, E. M., Morgan, P., & Lambert, E. (1995). Qualitative research considerations and other issues in the study of methamphetamine use among men who have sex with other men. In E. Lambert, R. Ashery, & R. Needle (Eds.), *Qualitative methods in drug abuse and HIV research* (NIDA Research Monograph 157, pp. 156-181). Rockville, MD: National Institute on Drug Abuse.

Gross, M., & Brown, V. (1993). Outreach to injection drug-using women. In B. Brown & G. Beschner (Eds.), *Handbook on risk of AIDS* (pp. 445-463). Westport, CT: Greenwood.

Humphreys, L. (1970). *Tearoom trade: Impersonal sex in public places.* Chicago: Aldine.

Hunt, D., Hammet, T., Smith, C., Rhodes, W., & Pares-Avila, J. (1993). Outreach to sex partners. In B. Brown & G. Beschner (Eds.), *Handbook on risk of AIDS* (pp. 464-482). Westport, CT: Greenwood.

Kane, S., & Mason, T. (1992). "IV drug users" and "sex partners": The limits of epidemiological categories and the ethnography of risk. In G. Herdt & S. Lindenbaum (Eds.), *The time of AIDS* (pp. 199-224). Newbury Park, CA: Sage.

Leonard, T. (1990). Male clients of female street prostitutes: Unseen partners in sexual disease transmission. *Medical Anthropology Quarterly, 4,* 41-55.

Lindesmith, A. (1947). *Opiate addiction.* Bloomfield, IN: Principia.

Marín, G., & Marín, B. V. (1991). *Research with Hispanic populations.* Newbury Park, CA: Sage.

Singer, M. (1993). Knowledge for use: Anthropology and community-centered substance abuse research. *Social Science and Medicine, 37,* 15-26.

Singer, M., & Marxuach-Rodriquez, L. (1996). Applying anthropology to the prevention of AIDS: The Latino Gay Men's Health Project. *Human Organization, 55,* 141-148.

Valdiserri, R. O. (1989). *Preventing AIDS: The design of effective programs.* New Brunswick, NJ: Rutgers University Press.

Watters, J., & Biernacki, P. (1989). Target sampling: Options for the study of hidden populations. *Social Problems, 36,* 416-430.

Webb, E., Campbell, T., Schwartz, B., & Sechrest, J. (1966). *Unobtrusive measures*. Chicago: Rand McNally.

Whyte, W. (1955). *Street corner society*. Chicago: University of Chicago Press.

Wiebel, W. (1990). Identifying and gaining access to hidden populations. In E. Lambert (Ed.), *The collection and interpretation of data from hidden populations* (National Institute on Drug Abuse Research Monograph Series #98, pp. 4-11). Rockville, MD: National Institute on Drug Abuse.

SUGGESTED RESOURCES

The study of hidden populations as a distinct field of research is an emergent field. Consequently, methodological literature in this arena is limited. The National Institute on Drug Abuse has issued a number of edited volumes in its Research Monograph Series that are especially germaine, including *The Collection and Interpretation of Data from Hidden Populations* (#98) and *Qualitative Methods in Drug Abuse and HIV Research* (#157). Similarly, the volume *Handbook on Risk of AIDS* includes a set of chapters on outreach approaches targeted to specific hidden populations. Articles by Watters and Biernacki (1989), Braunstein (1993), Clatts et al. (1995), and Carlson et al. (1994) each present thorough descriptions of the construction of targeted sampling plans in specific research settings.

INDEX

Absolute location, 105, 106
Acceptability in community organizations, 86-87
Access in hidden population research:
  and key informants, 15
  intrusive approaches to, 154-157
  unobtrusive approaches to, 154
Access to community organizations, types of, 86-87
Accessibility of community organizations, 86
Accommodation of community organization, 86-87
Accuracy:
  of database information, 106-107, 62 (table)
  of maps, 62 (table)
Acquaintance networks. *See* Convenience networks
Activity data, individual, analysis of, 80-82
Activity patterns, mapping, 108-109, 111-112, 108-112 (figures)
Activity records, 73-77
  data collection, 72, 73
Activity space, 69-70, 112-116
  as research task, 64 (table)
  data collection, 72-80
  defined, 69, 79
Actors, 34
Administrative region, 56-59
  boundaries of, as arbitrary, 57-59, 58 (figure), 59 (figure)
Affordability of community organizations, 86

Alters, 5
  data entry form for identifying, sample, 20 (figure)
  demographics and habits of, sample questionnaire, 22 (figure)
Analysis:
  data. *See* Data analysis
  spatial, xiv, 52
  units of, 51
ANTHROPAC, 50
Area, of a study. *See* Study area
Areal interpolation, 93
Area-weighting method, 93, 94 (figure), 95 (figure)
Artificial groups, 129
Attrition, 174-177
  effect on external validity, 180
Authority constraints, 68-69
Availability of community organizations, 86

Behavior:
  embedded, 15-17
  risk, 26-27
Behavior modification, 42
  social network approach to, 7
Beirnacki, P., 170
Ben Abdallah, A., 175-176
Bias:
  in hidden population research, 169-174
  in secondary data, 146, 147-148

in targeted sampling, 147
Bluthenthal, R., 157
Bolton, Ralph, 155-156
Bott, E., 3
Boundaries, 8-9
    of target populations, 141-143
Bounded groups, 8
Bridges, 7, 8-9
Brown, V., 128

C$_a$. See Coefficient of areal correspondence, 114
Cadastral maps, 63, 64 (table)
Capability constraint, 67
Capacity, and group identity, 133
Captive populations, 129
Cartographic, defined, 52
Cartographic paradox, 97-98
Cartography, computer. See Computer-assisted
    cartography
Central place theory, 85
Centrality, 84-85
Centralization, 32, 46
Chicago Model, 137-138, 140 (table)
Choropleth map, defined, 109
City directories, 63 (table), 64 (table)
Claverie, D., 175-176
Cliques/components, defined, 7, 30, 37
Cluster sampling, 96
Coefficient of areal correspondence (Ca), 114
Cognitive maps, defined, 70
Collection, data. See Data collection
Colocation, 68
Communication flow, in networks, 30-31, 32
Community, defined, 54-55
Community organizations, 83
    access to, types of, 86-87
    analysis, data, 90-94
    and governmental agencies, 87-88
    and private organizations, 88
    confidentiality and, 88-89, 93
    data collection, 86-90
    key informants and, 88
    size, 83
    spatial dimensions of, 83-94
    types of access to, 86-87
    variation in, 86
Community space, defined, 55
Compton, W., 175-176
Computer-assisted cartography, 100-102
    See also GIS

Confer, B., 175
Confidentiality:
    in community organization data collection,
        88-89, 93
    in mapping, 116, 117
    maintaining, in hidden populations,
        183-184
Connectedness, 30
Connectivity. See Information flow
Constraints, on human movement, 66-70
Contact records, in activity record, 73
Continuous comparison, 18
Continuous direct observation, 73-74
    alternatives to, 74-76
Convenience networks, 14
Copyright, 87
Cottler, L., 175-176
Coupling constraints, 68 (figure)
Critical approach, in social network interviewing,
    19-20 (figure)
Cross-group differences, 17-18

Dai, Bingham, 136
Daily time-space prism, 67, 67 (figure)
Data analysis:
    activity, individual, 80-82
    ego-centric network, 28-29
    mathematical programming models and,
        90-91
    network, 2, 25-26, 28-30, 33-36, 35 (figure),
        36 (figure)
    normative models and, 90-91, 92
    positive models and, 90
    spatial, 52-53, 53 (figure), 54 (figure)
Data collection:
    activity record, 72, 73
    activity space, 72-80
    cadastral maps and, 63 (table), 64 (table)
    city directories and, 63 (table), 64 (table)
    community organization, 86-90
    ego-centered network, 18-28, 19 (figure)
    full relational network, 33 (figure)
    sample of social networks matrix, 23 (figure)
    surveys, 41-42
    See also Data collection and mapping
Data collection and mapping, 62-65 (table)
Data recording matrix, 24 (figure)
Data sources, secondary, 146-149
Database, spatial, 103
    error, 106-107

Dayton Model, 138-139, 140 (table)
De Quincey, Thomas, 135
Density, 30
Desmond, D., 175
Deterministic models, *versus* stochastic process
    models, 82
Diaries, as activity space data collection method,
    72, 76
Disclosure laws, 88-89
    See also Confidentiality
Distortion, of maps. *See* Projection, map

Ecological approach, in social network
    interviewing, 19-20 (figure)
Edmundson, W. C., 74
Ego-centered networks, xiii, 5-6
Ego-centered network data:
    analysis, 25-26, 28-30
    types of, 5
    uses of, 6, 18, 27-28
Ego-centered network data collection, 18-28
    guide for, 19 (figure)
    questionnaires and, 18
    steps in, 28
Empathy, 164
Engels, Frederick, 135
Epidemiology, 137
Error. *See* Database spatial, error
Ethics:
    and spatial data use, 118
    in hidden population studies, xv-xvi
    See also Confidentiality; Disclosure laws;
        Referral, researcher; Research
        standards; Restrictions
Ethnography:
    of hidden populations, 149-150
    street, 137
    use of maps in, 103-104
Ethnography, applied, vii-viii
External validity, threats to, 179-181

Factions, 37, 46
Family-based networks, 12-13
Field model, 104
Field station, 166-169
    violence at, 186
Focal individuals, 5
Formal region, 56
Forward linkage, 85
Freedom of information, 87-88

Friendship-based networks. *See* Long-term
    friendship networks
Full relational social network, 6-7
Full relational social network data, 33-36, 33 (fig-
    ure), 35 (figure), 36 (figure)
Functional region, 56, 60-61, 61 (figure)

Game-based data collection, 72, 73
Gatekeepers, 44
Geocodes, latitude/longitude, 106
Geocoding, 105, 63 (table), 64 (table)
Geographic information systems. *See* GIS
GIS, 100-104, 106-107, 116 (figure)
    as means of surveillance and control, 118
    in hidden population studies, 148-149
Global positioning systems (GPS), 106
Going native, 155
GPS. *See* Global positioning systems
Graphic scales, in mapping, 98, 98 (figure)
Gross, M., 128
Gulick, J., 71

Hagerstrand, Torsten, 66-69
Hammet, T., 128-129
Hartford Model, 139-140, 140 (table)
Heterogeneity, of hidden populations, 173
Hidden population research:
    appeal of ethnographic approach in, 149-150
    evolution of, 135-140
    generalization of data in, 179-181
    key informants in, 150-151
    limiting bias in, 173-174
    methodology, 141-159
    participant observation and, 152-154
    recruiting problems in, 126
    sample size, 173
    sampling adequacy, 173
    sampling problems, 172-174
    secondary sources, 146-149
    use of GIS in, 148-149
    uses of, 127
    See also Attrition
Hidden populations, 125, 130-131
    confidentialty and, 183-184
    heterogeneity of groups in, 173
    importance of researching, 125-126
    locating, 43, 136-140
    recruiting, 126, 136. *See also* Participants,
        recruiting
    terminology for defining, 141-143, 172

types of, 128
Home base, 67
Homogeneity, in geographic regions, 56, 57, 58
Horne, M., 175-176
Humphrey, Laud, 155
Hunt, D., 128-129

Identity, group, 133
Identity hiding, 131-134
Imageability, of the environment, 70-71
Incentives, for study participants, 159, 161
Index individuals, 5
Informant, key, 150-153
Information flow, characterizations of, 30-31
Informed consent, 182
Institutional review board (IRB), 88
Institutions, community. *See* Community
    organizations
Integration, 85
Interaction, group, xii
Interaction research studies, 15-17
Interpretive approach, in social network
    interviewing, 19-20 (figure)
Interrater reliability, 178
Intervention, as threat to external validity, 181
Intervention programs, 3
    and network based outreach, 42, 43
Interviewer guide, for network data collection,
    19-20 (figure)
Interviewing, key informant, in hidden
    populations, 150-153
Interviews:
    focused group, ix
    social network, 19-20 (figure)
    IRB. *See* Institutional review board

Johnson, A., 75
Johnson, T., 175

Key informants:
    and collecting community organization data,
        90
    in hidden populations, 150-153

Lambert projection, 105
Leonard, Terri, 156-157
Lindesmith, Alfred, 136
Location, defined, 104
Location theory, in planning services, 91
Locational problems, as research task, 65 (table)

Longitudinal research:
    and travel time, 78
    design, xv
Long-term friendship networks, 13-14
Long-term injector networks, 12
Lynch, K., 70-71

Maddux, J., 175
Map comparison, 112-116
Map-making, 117
Mapping, 157-158
    ethics of, 118
    ethnographic network, 4-5
    See also Activity patterns, mapping;
        Hidden population research; Regions,
        geographical; Spatial data analysis
Maps, 97
    basic attributes of, 98-99
    chloropleth, 109, 110 (figure)
    cognitive, 70
    community-based research projects and,
        62-65 (table)
    confidentiality and, 116, 117
    dot density, 109, 110 (figure)
    existing, and data collection, 62 (table)
    graduated circle, 109, 110 (figure)
    in activity site research, 64 (table)
    in community organizations research,
        65 (table)
    insurance, 64 (table)
    locational problems research and, 65 (table)
    population distribution and, 63 (table)
    power of, 117-119
    restrictions on using, 62 (table)
    statistical, 100, 101 (figure)
    use of, to define study area, 62 (table)
Markov model, 82
Mercator projection, 105
Minnick, R. F., 114
Mobility, personal, 78, 91
Movement, human, constraints on, 66-69
MSM, 126
Multidimensional scaling, 115-116
Multiplex ties, 38

National Institute on Drug Abuse (NIDA), 137
Naturally occurring social network, 6
Neighborhood, defined, 71
Network relational data, uses of, 42
Network research, ethnographic:

advantages of, 42
in social network interviewing, 19-20 (figure)
steps in conducting, 17-18
uses of, 2, 5, 17
Network sampling, 2, 38-41
Network typologies, 9-15
drug, 11-15
uses of studies in, 9-10
Networks:
full relational (*See* Full relational social network)
mapping, 4-5
openness/closedness of, defined, 11
personal (*See* Ego-centered networks)
size and risk reduction, 46
NIDA. *See* National Institute on Drug Abuse
Nodes, in relational network studies, 40
Northeast Hispanic AIDS Consortium, 126

Object model of space, 104, 105 (figure)
Observations, in activity space data collection, 72
Obtrusive research methods, 154-156
Open network, 11
Orthophotos, digital, 106, 107 (figure)
Outreach, 159-160
network based, 43
Outreach workers:
as group member, 126
indigenous, 160
personal involvement of, 162-163
risk for, 164
training, 162, 164
Over-/undersampling, 148

Pares-Avila, J., 128-129
Participant observation, 152-154
Participants, recruitment of, 159-169
and network-based outreach, 43
incentives, 159, 161
mobile van approach (*See* Field station)
network, 165-166
order of, 27
street outreach, using, 159-164
Participants, retaining strategies, 175-177
See also Attrition
Pasternak, B., 3
Peer pressure, and behavior, 13, 16
Philadelphia Model, 139, 140 (table)
Photos, aerial, 63 (table), 64 (table)
Population, 127

membership, 129
patron, 129
target (*See* Hidden populations)
Populations, hidden. *See* Hidden populations
Positivistic approach, in social network interviewing, 19-20 (figure)
Power/influence, 30
Profiles, typical, in ego-centered networks, 5
Projection, map, 98-100, 99 (figure)
Proximity matrix, 115
Public health projects:
and hidden populations, 43
mobile service/clinic vans and, 167

Questionnaires:
alters, 20 (figure), 22 (figure)
in daily activity pattern data gathering, 76-77
in ego-centered network data collection, 18, 19 (figure)
Questions:
community organizations research, 65 (table)
for defining a study area using maps, 62 (table)
in activity site research, 64 (table)
in distribution of community members, 63 (table)
interview, 6-7, 19 (figure)
locational problems research, 65 (table)
typical, in full relational social networks, 6-7

Random walk design, in sampling, 41
Ratio scales, maps, 98, 98 (figure)
Reality, 70-71; *See also* Sense of place
Recall method, as activity space data record, 72, 76
problems with, 76-77
Reciprocal relationships within social networks, 30-38
uses of data collected in, 30
Recruitment, of study participants.
See Participants, recruitment of
Referral, by researcher, 185-186
Regions, geographical, 55, 56-59, 57 (figure)
concepts of, for defining a study area, 60
importance of studying, 58
Regular tesselation, 104, 104 (figure)
Relationship, changes, identifying, 31-32
Relative location, 105
Reliability, 177-179
Research standards, 181-182

Research techniques, audiovisual, ix
Researcher:
    and exposure to disease, 187-188
    and violence, xvi, 186-187
    as tool for collecting data, viii
    mobility, 77-78
    responsibilities of, to high risk participants,
        184-185
    role in social network interviewing,
        19 (figure)
    self-identification as group member, 155-157
    See also Ethics
Respondents and alters, comparison of, 2
    5 (table)
Restrictions:
    on data use, 87-89
    on database information usage, 62 (table)
    on map usage, 62 (table)
    See also Confidentiality; Disclosure laws;
        Ethics
Rhodes, W., 128-129
Risk, reducing, 44-45
Risk-taking, 27
Role relationships, 30

Sample:
    adequacy of, in hidden population research,
        173
    convenience, 171
    nonbiased, 172
    representative, 130
    size in hidden population research, 173
    variation in, ensuring, 136
Sampling:
    chain referral, 138
    focal, 79-80
    network, 2, 38-41
    spot, 77-79
    using random-walk design, 41
Sampling, spatial, 94-97
Sampling, targeted, 143-159
    steps in plan development, 144, 157-158
Sampling in space, 95-96
Sampling of space, 94-95
Sampling quota, proportional, 158
San Francisco Model, 138, 140 (table)
Satellite images, 63
Scale, map, 98, 98 (figure)
SDSS. See Spatial decision support systems, 92

Secondary sources. See Data sources, secondary
Semi-open networks, 13
Sense of place, 70, 71-72
Services, community, measuring, 89-90
Smith, C., 128-129
Social bond, 11
Social cohesion in groups, 31
Social concealment, 131-132
Social interactions, 11
Social network, 1, 36 (figure)
    diagram, 38
    naturally occurring, 6
Social network research, 3
    contemporary approaches to, 4-7
    uses of, 1-2, 3, 7
    See also Network, research, ethnographic
Social relations diagram. See Sociogram
Sociogram, 34, 35 (figure)
Space:
    community, 55
    field model of, 104
    object model of, 104
Space-time budgets, 66, 73
Spatial data, 51
Spatial data analysis, 52
    within ethnographic research, 52-53,
        53 (figure), 54 (figure)
Spatial data mapping, 97-116
Spatial database, 103
    error in, 106-107
Spatial decision support systems (SDSS), 92
Spatial perception, 70
Star pattern, 37-38
State plane coordinates, 105
States, in group analysis, 82
Statistical maps, 100, 101 (figure)
Stigmatization, 131-132
Stochastic process models, 82
Street outreach, 159-164
Structural equivalence in groups, 31
Studies:
    cross-sectional, xv
Study area, 55-56
    defining, 58-65, 62 (table)
Subgroups, in hidden population, 128
Surveillance, of individuals, practical problems
    with, 74-77
Surveys, types of, 41-42
Symbols, map, 100

variability in, 100, 102 (figure)
Sympathetic listening, 164

Targeted sampling plan:
mapping boundaries of, 145
using secondary data in, 146-149
Targeted sampling strategy, 138
Tesselation, regular, 104, 104 (figure)
Threshold requirements, service facilitie, 83-85, 92
Ties, 26
Time allocation studies. *See* Time use studies
Time budgets, 66, 73
Time use studies, 66
travel time in, 78
Time-space, of a community, 55
Topographic maps, 100
Tracking network members, 43-44
Transgendered individuals, 132
Trash can addicts, 14
Travel records as activity records, 73

Typologies:
how ethnographers generate, 9
uses of, 10

UCINET IV, 50
Unobtrusive research methods, 154

Valdiserri, Ronald, 162
Validity, 178, 179-181
Variation:
cultural, within groups, 9
in hidden population, types of, 130
in samples, ensuring, 136
temporal, in activity studies, 79-80
Violence, in the field, 186
See also Researcher
Voluntary associations, 17

Watters, J., 157, 170
Weak ties, 12, 26
Whyte, William F., 151

ABOUT THE AUTHORS, ARTISTS, AND EDITORS

Ellen K. Cromley is a medical geographer who studies geographical patterns of human health and disease, geographical location of health services and factors that affect their utilization, and medical mapping using geographic information systems. She earned a BA in urban and environmental studies from Case Western Reserve University, an MA in geography from Ohio State University, and a PhD in geography from the University of Kentucky. Her current research projects, conducted with staff of the Connecticut Departments of Public Health and Environmental Protection, use geographic information systems to support emerging infectious disease surveillance, analysis of motor vehicle collisions, and regulation of public drinking water supplies.

Jean J. Schensul is a medical/educational anthropologist. After completing her M.A. and Ph.D. at the University of Minnesota, she conducted intervention research in education at the Institute for Juvenile Research and Center for New Schools in Chicago. She served as co-founder and research director of the Hispanic Health Council in Hartford for ten years, and, since 1987, has been founder and executive director of the Institute for Community Research, based in Hartford, Connecticut, and dedicated to community-based partnership research. She has extensive experience in the use of ethnographic and survey research methods in the United States, Latin America, Southeast Asia, China, and West Africa. Her substantive interests are diverse, reflecting the contributions of ethnography to health, education, the arts, and community development. She co-edited three special journal issues on applied research in education, and policy, and, with Don Stull, a book titled *Collaborative Research and Social Change: Applied Anthropology in Action*, and has published on other topics including substance abuse prevention, AIDS, adolescent development, chronic health problems, and the arts and community building. She is the recipient of a number of National Institute of Health Research grants, immediate past president of the Society for Applied Anthropology, former president of the Council on Anthropology and Education, and recipient (with Stephen Schensul) of the Kimball Award for Public Policy Research in Anthropology. She is Adjunct Professor of Anthropology at the University of Connecticut and Senior Fellow, Department of Psychology, Yale University.

Merrill Singer is a medical anthropologist who specializes in the applied study of inner-city health issues. As the Associate Director and Chief of Research at the Hispanic Health Council in Hartford, Connecticut, and as Associate Clinical Professor in the Department of Community Medicine, University of Connecticut Health Center, he directs or codirects a set of projects that addresses HIV risk among drug users, the relationship between drug use and violence, emergent patterns of drug use, and the role of syringe exchange in HIV risk reduction. He has published more than 100 articles in health and social science journals and as book chapters, and is coauthor or editor of *Medical Anthropology and the World System* (1997), *The Political Economy of AIDS* (1997), *Critical Medical Anthropology* (1995), and *African American Religion in the 20th Century* (1992). He has served as Chairman of the American Anthropological Association Taskforce on AIDS and as a member of the American Anthropology Association Commission on AIDS, the Executive Committee of the Society for Applied Anthropology, the Executive Committee of the National Association of Professional Anthropologists, the AIDS and Behavior Grant Review Committee of the National Institute on Drug Abuse, and the Executive Committee of the Center for the Interdisciplinary Research on AIDS at Yale University. He has also been Associate Editor of the journal *Medical Anthropology*.

Margaret D. LeCompte is Professor of Education and Sociology in the School of Education, University of Colorado at Boulder. After completing her MA and PhD at the University of Chicago, she taught at the University of Houston and the University of Cincinnati, with visiting appointments at the University of North Dakota and the Universidad de Monterrey, Mexico. She also served as Executive Director for Research and Evaluation for the Houston public schools. In addition to many articles and book chapters, she coauthored *Ethnography and Qualitative Design in Educational Research* and coedited the *Handbook of Qualitative Research in Education*, the first textbook and first handbook on ethnographic and qualitative methods in education. As a researcher, evaluator, and consultant to school districts, museums, and universities, she has published studies of dropouts, artistic and gifted students, school reform efforts, and the impact of strip mining on the social environment of rural communities. Fluent in Spanish, she is deeply interested in language education and the education of ethnic minority children. She served as a Peace Corps volunteer in the Somali Republic from 1965 to 1967.

Robert T. Trotter II is an Arizona Regents' Professor in the Department of Anthropology at Northern Arizona University. His primary research interests are in cross-cultural health care research and in finding ways of making health care systems more compatible with differing cultural beliefs. He has worked on traditional healing, migrant health in the United States, alcohol and drug programs, AIDS prevention, and the revision of the International Classification of Impairments, Disabilities and Handicaps. He is interested in finding ways of using advanced ethnographic research methods in applied anthropology projects.

Ed Johnetta Miller is a weaver/silk painter/gallery curator/ quilter and Master Teaching Artist. Her work has appeared in the *New York Times* and *FiberArts Magazine* and in the Renwick Gallery of the Smithsonian, American Crafts Museum, and Wadsworth Atheneum. She is the Director of OPUS, Inc., Co-Director of the Hartford Artisans Center, and consultant to Aid to Artisans, Ghana. She teaches workshops on weaving, silk painting and quilting to children and adults throughout the United States.

Graciela Quiñones Rodriguez is a folk artist, carving *higueras* (gourds) and working in clay, wood, and lithographs with symbols and icons derived from Taino and other indigenous art forms. She builds *cuatros, tiples,* and other Puerto Rican folk instruments guided by the inspiration of her grandfather Lile and her uncle Nando who first introduced her to Puerto Rican cultural history and Taino culture and motifs. Her work has been exhibited in major galleries and universities thoughout Connecticut, at the Bridgeport Public Library, at the Smithsonian Institute.